Reclaim Her
HEART

**Empowering Moms to Raise Teen Daughters with
Kingdom Identity in a World of Conformity**

Praise

"The best way to raise a generation of girls who have found true beauty and confidence in Christ is to equip their mothers to do the same. In Reclaim Her Heart, Trudy Lonesky uses a perfect blend of vulnerability, relatability, scripture, and biblical encouragement to touch and transform a mother's heart."

- Heather Creekmore.
Body image expert, podcast host, and author of Compared to Who? and The Burden of Better

"Reclaim Her Heart" equips moms to walk securely in their God-given identity and value and encourages them on their journey of raising set apart and confident girls who love Jesus and know their worth.

- Allie Marie Smith
Author of "Wonderfully Made: Discover the Identity, Love, and Worth You Were Created For" and the Founder and Director of Wonderfully Made®

"In order for us moms to encourage and uplift our daughters, we need to reflect on our own experiences to authentically minister to them. Trudy Lonesky helps us explore our own memories of past challenges so we can receive affirmation and healing from the Lord. Then we will be better equipped to help our daughters become women of faith.

- Sarah Geringer
Christian writer, creative coach, book launch manager, artist, podcaster, and author of several books, including Transforming Your Thought Life for Teens.

Reclaim Her
HEART

**Empowering Moms to Raise Teen Daughters with
Kingdom Identity in a World of Conformity**

TRUDY LONESKY

Arabelle Publishing, LLC
Chesterfield, Virginia

Reclaim Her Heart
Empowering Moms to Raise Teen Daughters
with Kingdom Identity in a World of Conformity
Copyright @2022 Trudy Lonesky

Published by Arabelle Publishing, LLC
Chesterfield, Virginia
www.arabellebooks.com
IG: @arabellepublishing
IG: @arabellebooks

Cover Design by Samuel Rog
Interior Design by Jennie Lyne Hiott @bookcoverit.com

Library of Congress Control Number: 2022938876

Printed in the United States of America, 2022
ISBN: 9-781735-632872

Group Sales:
Books are available with special quantity discounts when purchased in bulk directly from the publisher. This discount applies to corporations, organizations, and special interest groups. For more information, email the publisher at arabellepublishing@gmail.com

*To my Little Lola Love,
it's been a pleasure to see God work in your life.
You are the inspiration for this book.*

Contents

Introduction 1
Day 1 3
Day 2 11
Day 3 17
Day 4 23
Day 5 31
Day 6 39
Day 7 47
Day 8 55
Day 9 63
Day 10 71
Day 11 79
Day 12 87
Day 13 93
Day 14 99
Day 15 105
Day 16 111
Day 17 119
Day 18 127
Day 19 135
Day 20 141
Day 21 149
Day 22 157
Day 23 165
Day 24 171
Day 25 179

Day 26. 187
Day 27. 193
Day 28. 201
Day 29. 209
Day 30. 215
Conclusion. 221
About the Author. 222

Introduction

Dear friend,

Can I call you that if we've never met? If you have this book in hand, I know you're looking for support, love, and encouragement in preserving the beautiful, childlike faith that exists within your sweet daughter's heart. Or maybe you are looking to restore brokenness and pain she has endured. Regardless of why you purchased this book, I am walking alongside you as a sister in Christ, excited to empower you to live in complete confidence in God's plan for your family.

I birthed this book out of an epiphany. It was Labor Day, September 2, 2019. I knew God was calling me to lead tween and teen girls. However, I sought worldly approval through social media, my body image, and my personal appearance. My workouts came before my time with God. I was obsessed with the number on the scale, weighing myself daily—and the number was never low enough.

Then I heard God whisper, "Trudy, how can I allow you to lead My girls if you aren't seeking Me first? It's time to lay it all down at the foot of the cross."

The tears began to flow and I fell to my knees. On that day, I began a journey of complete and total surrender. It didn't happen overnight, and I am not saying I get it right every day. There are days I get caught up scrolling social, seeking approval through likes, comments, and shares. It's a constant heart check and posture change. *All of me, God. All for You. Your Kingdom come; my Kingdom go.*

Through this process, I realized that where I find my identity, value, and worth will determine where my daughter finds hers. That was a hard pill to swallow. I could spend the rest of my days allowing my girl to watch her mother miserably seek the ways of this world, or I could be a witness to her young, impressionable heart. My choices will affect the way she sees this world. My behavior needs to reflect a very real Jesus living within me.

As parents/mentors, we are navigating newfound territory in the lives of the girls around us. There has never been more pressure to measure up in appearance, academics, and athletics. Social media invites our girls to a public competition of self-worth. If left to their own wandering hearts, they will look for validation and worth in places and spaces that will leave them feeling empty inside.

Helping our daughters maneuver through the minefield of modern life starts by addressing the struggles of our own hearts.

Friend, I am not sure where your struggles lie, but I know that God knows. With Him, we can rise above the societal pressures and norms to fit in as moms, and we can reposition our priorities to seek God for the good and the glory of our families. We get to lay down the striving and sit confidently in His good and perfect plan for our lives. In doing so, we empower the next generation of Kingdom daughters to rise and glorify Him in all they do.

I love you, sister. God loves you. We've got Kingdom work to do.

In Him,

Your sister in Christ

Day 1

Daughter of the King: Identity

But you are a chosen race, a royal priesthood, a holy nation, a people for his own possession, that you may proclaim the excellencies of him who called you out of darkness into his marvelous light.

1 Peter 2:9 NIV

"On my darkest of days when I feel inadequate, unloved, and unworthy, I remember whose daughter I am, and I straighten my crown."

~Unknown

I fought for the need to be seen, validated, and enough for much of my life. I had deep-seated feelings of inadequacy, which were rooted in my childhood. I was the less fortunate child—flying under the radar, barely seen, unwanted, unloved, a mistake. I spent hours in the gym each day in my early twenties and tried countless diets. I tried to find my identity and worth in the scale and pant size, only to fall short. Fast forward to motherhood, and I wanted to be the Pinterest mom, sending my kids to school with nothing but the best, well-thought-out school projects. I felt the need to prove myself to everyone I encountered.

Recently, God showed me that I was trying to find my identity in all the wrong things. I discovered that only God could heal the brokenness within my heart, remove the labels others had placed on me, and tell me who I truly am. The same is true for you, sweet sister. No matter what others have said about you, God is the only one who determines your

3

identity and worth. Striving can't and won't fill the void we so longingly attempt to fill. It never will. Our brokenness can only be mended and pieced back together by our loving Father in Heaven. He knows our pain. He hurts with us and for us. He sees our bruised, battered, and fragile hearts, and His love surrounds us right where we are.

As women, we constantly strive to do, be, create. We want to have influence, be seen, feel important, worthy, valued. I have spent a good portion of my life needing to feel like what I have done matters, constantly striving to feel successful. But for who? Where I choose to place my sense of self becomes subjective when I allow the world to determine who I am. God never intended others to define who we are and who we were created to be. Only He has the authority to do so.

Sweet friend, what if all that He has created us to be is right here in this moment where we are already placed? What if He made us for such a time as this—mothering these children, raising the next generation in the way they should go, and ensuring kingdom values in our children for a thousand generations to come?

Dear friend, when we are at peace with our God-given identity within our own hearts, we invite our daughters to do the same. Our girls are watching us closely. They will mimic our attitudes, heart postures, and beliefs. When we lay down the striving and pick up the perfect peace of our identity in Him, we empower our girls to live their lives according to His call that He has placed over them as well.

Sister friend, you are more than a conqueror. Fierce in the eyes of the Lord. Made for such a time as this. Chosen. Royalty. Daughter of the King. Chin up. Fix your crown.

GO DEEPER:

God calls you and knows you by name. We've been adopted into His royal priesthood, and that, sweet sister, makes you royalty. In 1 Peter 2:9, Peter says that because we are fully known and called by God, He calls us out of the darkness and into *His marvelous light.* HIS light. Not a light we can grasp anywhere else, but only His. I don't know about you, sweet mama, but I find that encouraging. God is specific about where we need to find our identity: in Him and only Him.

We are God's chosen people, just like the Israelites were in the OT (Old Testament). As a Christian, we inherit the same promises God gave Israel. We can look back in the Old Testament and see those identities He gave us.

In Exodus 19:5-6, "Now if you obey me fully and keep my covenant, then out of all nations you will be my treasured possession. Although the whole earth is mine, you will be for me a kingdom of priests and a holy nation. These are the words you are to speak to the Israelites." As His treasured possession, we can live in confidence that we are loved, adopted, pleasing to God.

Deuteronomy 4:20 states, "But as for you, the Lord took you and brought you out of the iron-smelting furnace, out of Egypt, to be the people of his inheritance, as you now are." As Jesus' followers, we have inherited the kingdom of God. We have all we need because of the inheritance He has given us.

"For you are a people holy to the Lord your God. The Lord, your God, has chosen you out of all the peoples on the face of the earth to be his people, his treasured possession." Deuteronomy 7:6

"The wild animals honor me,
the jackals and the owls,
because I provide water in the wilderness
and streams in the wasteland,
to give drink to my people, my chosen,
the people I formed for myself
that they may proclaim my praise."

Isaiah 43:20-21.

When we stand confidently in our God-given identity and purpose, we can give Him glory and praise. God never intended for us to look elsewhere for value and recognition. Our approval has already been won by the blood of Jesus.

Reflect

Where are you tempted to find identity? In what areas do you strive? Ask God to meet you in those spaces and help you find peace in those areas. Write a prayer asking that He fill the emptiness with His lovingkindness and remind you who you are in Him. Ask Him how He sees you. You might just be surprised and encouraged by His answer.

♥ Conversation Starters ♥

What lies have you believed about your identity? Where are you tempted to place your identity outside of God? What are some labels that people call you? What are some labels that you call yourself?

Pray

Father God, thank You for reminding me today that I am Your possession. Thank You for showing up in the middle of my brokenness and pain. Lord, when my heart wants to believe the lies that others place on me or even the lies I put on myself, give me the strength and courage to turn toward Your radiant light instead. God, I know in my heart of hearts that I am who You say I am and nothing else. Help me lay my heavy heart down at Your feet, Lord. Thank You for the gift of motherhood. Give me the courage, strength, and grit to raise this (these) girl (s) in uncertain times. I know I can do all things through You because You are the source of my strength. Thank You for Your ever-present help.
In Jesus' name, I pray. Amen.

Day 2

Worth More than Rubies: Worthiness

Before I formed you in the womb I knew you,
before you were born I set you apart.

Jeremiah 1:5 NIV

Friend, you are ridiculously loved, set apart, chosen, and created for a purpose. God saw the world He had created and thought it was missing one thing. That one thing was you. You are created in His image and adopted into His royal priesthood. That means you are royalty, heir to the kingdom that awaits you in Heaven.

Let go of the feelings of being less than and not enough. You don't need to look at other women and wish you were them, look like them, or covet all they have. Your worth is not determined by the car you drive, the place you call home, the label on the purse you carry, the validation of others, or how much money is in your bank account. You are placed where you are on purpose for such a time as this.

Where we find our worth will absolutely determine where our daughters find theirs. Girl, I challenge you to live boldly in the promise that you are set apart. You are not meant to follow the status quo; you are made to be different, live differently, and love differently. Will you set aside any temptation to find worthiness outside of Him? Will you stand confidently in your worth so you can equip your daughter (s) to do the same?

God encourages you and has given you permission to be the beautiful masterpiece He has created. In fact, He invites you to do so. He doesn't want you to be anyone other than you! We model peace and assurance for generations of girls when we get this right.

GO DEEPER:

In Jeremiah 1:5, God spoke to Jeremiah and reassured him He had a specific plan and purpose over Jeremiah's life. To be a prophet to the nations. God knows us, and He calls us by name. As Christians, we all have a plan and purpose, just as Jeremiah did.

Let's take a step back and look at some of the plans He had over the women of the bible. He called Deborah in Judges 4:4-5, the only female judge to Israel, to be a prophet and heroine and inspire the Israelites to overcome the oppression of the Canaanites. They had oppressed Israel for 20 years. She could have easily questioned her worth as a woman. She could have questioned God's prompting and her call. However, she was available to God, never questioned her authority, and rose to the challenge. She eventually delivered her people because she believed in who God called her to be.

God called Esther to save the Jews from Haman's evil schemes. She risked her life to approach King Xerxes on behalf of her people, the Jews. The bible doesn't say that Esther questioned her authority in consulting the King. Even though she was queen, going before a king without being called was dangerous. God prompted Esther to take action, and she did. It was because of her that her people were delivered from a massacre.

Set apart. What does that mean for you, friend? That means that you are called to be different. To walk in a confidence that is not brought on by anything that the world can give you but comes from who you are in God. The next time you question your worthiness, take a step back and ask yourself what is causing you to question your worth. Stand confident in what God sees when He looks at you. Set apart. Worthy. Loved. Chosen. Forgiven.

Reflect

Take a few moments to consider what makes you feel unworthy. Have some situations made you question who you are? Now let's flip the script. Who does God say you are? Take some time and ask Him in prayer, "God, who do You say I am?" The next time you question your worthiness, remind yourself of who you are—God's perfect, glorious masterpiece.

♥ Conversation Starters ♥

What makes you feel worthy? Are there times when you feel like you are not enough? If so, when do you feel this way? Do you believe God has set you apart? Do you understand the magnitude of that statement?

Pray

Father God, thank You for creating me in Your Image. Thank You for making me the unique, beautiful, intelligent, worthy girl I am today. Help me be unapologetically myself. When I am tempted to be someone else or feel the need to fit in, remind me that I am enough because You don't make mistakes. In Jesus' name, I pray. Amen.

Day 3

The Joy Thief: Comparison

The LORD is my shepherd. I lack nothing.

Psalm 23:1 NIV

"Comparison is the thief of joy."

~Theodore Roosevelt

In today's world, it's easy to compare ourselves to others. If we are completely honest, we've probably spent at least two-thirds of our life looking at the world and measuring our successes or failures against someone else's. Many of us feel like we are constantly competing with families around us. We are tempted to be the perfect Pinterest mom, ensuring that our child's science project surpasses the other children's projects. We compare our children's athletic and academic performances to those of other children. We go through life tirelessly, putting on a facade that we have it all and that we have it all together.

Friend, when I feel like I don't measure up and I think someone else has it all together, I've learned that the person I am comparing myself with often has their own feelings of insecurity. Someone may look like they have it together, but deep inside, they could be falling apart. When seeds of inadequacy begin to take root in your heart, remind yourself that you lack nothing. We serve a very intentional God who provides us with everything we need.

Get your blinders on. Keep your eyes laser-focused on yourself, God, the blessings before you, and the provision God has given you. We lack nothing because our heavenly Father loves us, and He will provide for our every need.

We are in this world, but we are not of this world. The clothes we wear, the friends we keep, or the pant size we wear does not measure our worthiness. God sees us in a whole new light. In the eyes of the world, we may not measure up, but in the eyes of our Father, we have it all. Jesus paid for it all for us to spend eternity with Him. In His eyes, we were worth dying for.

GO DEEPER

Our God is faithful, sister. He will provide for our every need like the good shepherd that He is. So good, in fact, that He sent His son to die on a cross so that we can experience eternity. Philippians 4:19, TPT, says, "I am convinced that my God will fully satisfy every need you have, for I have seen the abundant riches of glory revealed to me through Jesus Christ!" Every need. That isn't a desire, or the desire to be or have something that someone else possesses, but every need that God knows we must have.

What is at the heart of comparison? Worldly approval. If I have what she has or looks like she does, I will be loved, accepted, valued. God asks us to turn those thoughts to Him. Galatians 1:10 says, "Am I now trying to win the approval of human beings, or of God? Or am I trying to please people? If I were still trying to please people, I would not be a servant of Christ."

Comparison brings condemnation. Sister, there is no condemnation in Christ Jesus (Romans 8:1). When we allow comparison to penetrate our thought life, it will take our joy from us. The Lord is our Shepherd, our Provider, our Comforter, an ever-present help in times of need. Because He provides for us, we lack absolutely nothing. Find sweet comfort in His love for you. You are perfect the way you are. No one will ever compare to you.

Reflect

*T*he Lord is our Shepherd, and therefore we lack nothing. Write a thank-you note to God below. How has He provided for you? What blessings has He given you?

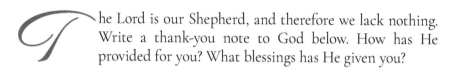

♥ *Conversation Starters* ♥

In what areas do you find that you compare yourself to others? When do you feel unworthy or that you don't measure up to those around you? If social media causes most of your joy thieving, it might be time to unfollow or "mute" accounts that leave you feeling less than.

_____

_____

_____

_____

_____

_____

_____

_____

_____

_____

_____

_____

_____

_____

_____

_____

_____

_____

_____

_____

_____

_____

_____

Pray

Father God, I know there is no condemnation in Christ Jesus. When I feel the need to compare my life and circumstances to others, Lord remind me that You and You alone are enough. I lack and am worthy. I am unconditionally loved and fearfully and wonderfully made. I need nothing from this world because I am fulfilled. In Jesus' name, I pray. Amen.

Day 4

Peace be Still: Anxiety

For God hath not given us the spirit of fear; but of power, and of love, and of a sound mind.

2 Timothy 1:7 KJV

What keeps you up at night? What worries do you hold on to? What disrupts your peace and steals your joy? As mothers, our hearts and minds are prone to wander. Elizabeth Stone once said, "deciding to have a child—it is momentous. It is to decide forever to have your heart go walking around outside your body." That quote gets me every time because it is oh so true.

Having a child can bring a myriad of worries and fears. When our children are babies, we fear they won't meet their milestones. Will they meet the benchmarks of crawling, walking, talking? As they grow into preschool, we fear we haven't taught them enough. Do they know their ABCs? Are they reading ready? In grade school, we might fear choosing the wrong school or making bad educational choices. Those are just parenting-related fears and anxieties; add work, social life, and marriage to the mix, and we have been given an invitation straight from the enemy to drown in a sea of anxious thoughts.

I'm afraid that my child will choose the wrong path.
I fear that I will never measure up at work.
I am anxious that my husband will have an affair.
I'm afraid that I've failed to parent my children.

Your anxious, wandering heart, if left to its own devices, will lead you astray. God will never give you a spirit of fear... ever. He won't put any fearful thoughts in your head, my friend. Fearful and anxious thoughts are not meant to replay over and over in your mind. Fear is a liar. What you do with those fears and anxieties matters. We can choose to entertain them or take them captive and unpack them by asking ourselves questions: Where are these thoughts coming from? What does God say about them? Are they true, noble, kind, praiseworthy? If not, call those thoughts what they are: lies straight from the enemy himself. Use Scripture to help you process the fear. Hold on to God's truth instead of the lies the enemy is feeding you.

When you feel like all hope is lost, pray. Give it to God. "Cast all your anxiety on him because he cares for you" (1 Peter 5:7). Stand on the truth that God is in whatever circumstance you're facing and that He will work all things out for your good. He is in the waiting, sister. Praise Him in the middle of your circumstances and the overwhelming fear you face. In time, He will reveal Himself to you. Eventually, you will look back and be in awe of how He showed up and worked in and through your anxious heart.

Sweet friend, stand confident in His plan because God has made a way into your life before, and He will do it again.

GO DEEPER

In the books of 1st and 2nd Timothy, Paul addresses Timothy himself. Paul saw the fear and lies the enemy was feeding Timothy. God spoke through Paul, and he addressed Timothy's fear. He wanted Timothy to know that the lies the enemy was feeding him weren't of God. Neither are they for you, sweet sister.

To address fear in our own hearts and minds, we must first discern the truth. Are the words we are hearing from God? Would He give us those thoughts? Are they true, noble, kind, praiseworthy?

Second, we must consider what God has given us. What is He instilling in us if He isn't giving us fearful thoughts? God gives us power. Do you believe that with your whole heart, sister friend? There is so much power in His name. In fact, the bible says, "The name of the Lord is a strong tower; the righteous man runs into it and is safe." Proverbs 18:10 ESV He is our safe place. He also gives us love. A love so deep that we see the world through a love-filtered lens. We can love others boldly because Jesus was a perfect example of that love while here on earth.

Lastly, He has given us a sound mind. This means our thoughts are calm, collected, and biblically focused. We don't have to give into the anxieties and fears because our thoughts are driven by God's truths.

I used the King James Version for our key verse because I love the words this version uses to empower us, particularly the term "sound mind." Fears and anxieties will run rampant through our minds if we allow them to. When we realize God doesn't give us those thoughts, we are empowered to take those thoughts captive and rewrite our script (our stories). God gives us the opposite of fear. He gives us the spirit of power, love (unconditional, all-powerful, abundant love), and a sound mind (the ability to decipher between truth and lies).

Reflect

Can you think of a "But God" moment? A moment when you felt hopeless, but God showed up with a bigger and better plan than you had ever imagined? Journal about that time in the space below. How does this "But God" moment inspire you in your current trials and circumstances?

♥ Conversation Starters ♥

What recent or current fears are you facing? Where do you think these fears might come from? What is the worst-case scenario if these worries were to come true? Will it matter in 5, 10, 15 years? How can I help you rewrite those fears and align them with what God says about them?

_____
_____
_____
_____
_____
_____
_____
_____
_____
_____
_____
_____
_____
_____
_____
_____
_____
_____
_____
_____
_____
_____
_____

Pray

Father God, I thank You for the reminder that I don't need to carry my burdens on my own. You are in the waiting, and I know that when I feel scared, stuck, and hopeless, You are working to make all things new according to Your good and perfect plan. Help me stand in confidence that You will show up in my circumstances because You have done so before, and You promise to do so again. I thank You, Lord, for Your faithfulness. Thank You for never leaving me or forsaking me. In Jesus' name, I pray. Amen.

Day 5

Wonderfully Made: Finding Your Worth in God

For You formed my inward parts;
You wove me in my mother's womb.
I will give thanks to You, for I am fearfully and wonderfully made;
Wonderful are Your works,
And my soul knows it very well.

Psalm 139:13-14 NIV

You are fearfully and wonderfully made. Friend, do you believe that in your heart of hearts? God knit you in your mother's womb, and He said what He created was oh so good. Yet, just like the enemy tempted Eve to take her eyes off God in the Garden of Eden (Genesis 3:11), he tempts us today. He finds joy in keeping us from being the women God has created us to be. He wants to keep us busy and preoccupied instead of living in God's truths. He tempts us to find worth in all the wrong things — in the busyness of our schedule, in the approval of those around us, or in the clothing we wear.

But God never intended for us to seek fullness in the things that this world offers. Trust me when I say that I have spent much of my life trying to feel like I was worthy of love and approval. I found that striving would bring me temporary gain, but it could never satisfy the longing to be enough. In my self-effort, God always brought me back to Him, His still small voice reminding me that I was created to be enough the moment I was conceived.

Friend, you are fierce, a mighty warrior in the eyes of God. You can do all things *through Him* because He is the source of your strength. You don't need to look to anyone else for validation because your validation was fought for and won on the cross. Jesus gave it all so that you could live in complete assurance of who you were created to be.

Where you find your worth will absolutely determine how you see yourself AND how your daughter sees herself. Your confidence in who you are is dependent on where you find your identity. God never meant for us to search anywhere else but Him. You are worthy. You are fearfully and wonderfully made in the eyes of the God of all creation. And sister, that is enough.

Lay down the striving and breathe in the beauty of His creation that is you, my friend.

GO DEEPER

The moment God created us, He instilled His character within us. We are worthy because He lives in us. Don't miss this, sweet sister. The Lord of all creation is within you, yes you. That's humbling, right? He is the potter, and we are the clay, as Isaiah 64:8 states. It wasn't by accident that we are alive on this planet. He was highly intentional when He created us.

"You formed my innermost being,
shaping my delicate inside and my intricate outside,
And wove them all together in my mother's womb."

TPT

The Hebrew word for "wove" or "knit" used in some bible translations of this verse means "covered" or "defended." Not only did He create us, but He also sent guardian angels to watch over us. We are so special to Him, so worthy in fact that He has us covered and protected.

That you were born is a miracle straight from God Himself. Tiny, intricate cells work simultaneously together to form you. God uniquely knit you in your mother's womb. He created you and called you His. He says you are worth more than rubies, priceless and hard to find. Stand in complete confidence that you are worthy, loved, and precious in the eyes of your Heavenly Father. So worthy, in fact, you were worth dying for.

Let's go a bit deeper into Psalms 139. In verses 16-18, it states,
"Your eyes saw my unformed body;
all the days ordained for me were written in your book
before one of them came to be.
How precious are your thoughts concerning me, God.
How vast is the sum of them!"

Let's summarize. God formed us uniquely in our mother's womb. He has specifically numbered our days. And He thinks so highly of us. He calls us holy and blameless in His sight (Ephesians 1:4). We aren't an accident or a mistake. In fact, we were created very much on purpose for His glory.

When you stand in that confidence with your whole heart, your daughter can't help but see and want that very same thing for herself. You are worthy, and so is your sweet girl. Bask in the goodness of that promise today.

TRUDY LONESKY

Reflect

W rite a letter to yourself. I know you may have just rolled your eyes at me. Trust me. Write an acceptance letter to yourself. Apologize for the times you didn't love who you are. Make amends. Quote any Scripture that reaffirms who God says you are.

♥ Conversation Starters ♥

> **Where might you be searching for worthiness? Do you feel like you have ever achieved worthiness on your own? What does God say about the creation that is you? He calls you by name and knows the number of hairs on your head. How does that make you feel?**

34

Pray

Dear heavenly Father, help me love myself the way You love me. Remind me that You are creating me was not an accident. In fact, it was very much on purpose and planned. Help me understand that the mere formation of me was a miracle. When I am tempted to find validation in moving targets, remind me where I stand with You. Lord, I know in my heart that I am fearfully and wonderfully made because it is written in the Bible. Help me believe that when my heart wanders. In Jesus' name, I pray. Amen.

Day 6

So Long Insecurities: Overcoming Insecurities

Whoever dwells in the shelter of the Most High
will rest in the shadow of the Almighty.

Psalm 91:1 NIV

Past hurts and insults leave deep wounds of insecurity. If you're anything like me, you can look back through your life and remember when things were said or done to you that left scars. When we leave those wounds open and perhaps entertain the words that have been spoken over us, we allow ourselves to take on identities that God never meant for us to carry.

When I was a young girl, I was extremely self-conscious about the gap between my front teeth. I became even more insecure about this aspect of my appearance when my classmates started making fun of me about it. When I spoke or smiled, they would snicker.

Teasing and taunting about how I looked and other personal characteristics took a toll on my tender heart as a young girl. The criticism came from several sources, which I interpreted to mean what was being said about me was true. After a while, I held the lies as gospel. What others said about me dug a deep-sea of insecurity into my tender little heart. Each dig chipped away at my identity and self-confidence.

Soon, the insecurities were so ingrained that I didn't even know who I was anymore. I masked the insecurity by dressing nicely, covering up with makeup, and putting on a facade that just wasn't me. I built walls to protect myself and wouldn't let anyone in, even those who loved me the most. I was left fragile and broken, wondering how much more I could take.

BUT GOD...

In His perfect timing, He revealed to me exactly who I was in Him. Those flaws that everyone pointed out were real blessings. The criticism only made me stronger. I am thankful for my persecutors and the naysayers because those trials allowed me to lean into my heavenly Father, trusting that He made me perfect in His beautiful image. He doesn't make mistakes. *I am not a mistake*. I was created intentionally to fulfill His purpose on this planet.

Insecurity. In its most profound sense, it is pride. When we choose to be insecure, we give too much power to the thought that others are judging us. Maybe they are, perhaps they aren't. Regardless, to give those thoughts weight to how we carry ourselves isn't what God intended for us.

Friend, you were created in this world, but you are not of it. As Jesus' followers, we are called to walk differently. Our confidence and security must come from Him. When we fix our eyes on Him and see ourselves through His eyes, we will find courage and confidence to be ourselves — fully loved and accepted as daughters of the King.

GO DEEPER

Psalm 91 in its entirety is powerful. The Passion Translation is my favorite version of this chapter. I challenge you to open your bible and read the whole chapter. Verse 1 says, "Whoever dwells in the shelter of the Most High will rest in the shadow of the Almighty." When we dwell in Him and find security and refuge in Him, we will find peace. We need to allow God and God alone to be our shelter. Not the opinions of others or the gaping wounds we carry.

While the author of this chapter is unknown, some say that Moses wrote it while wandering in the wilderness. Let's say it was Moses. He faced many obstacles; lack of food and water, grumbling from the Israelites, warring tribes coming at them (the Amalekites). However, Moses chose to fix his eyes on the Lord, and we can too.

While our trials and feelings of persecution may not be as extreme as what Moses endured, it encourages us to have perspective. To find shelter in the God who created us (verse 1) and place our security in

Him (verse 2). Letting go of any labels (verse 3) has left wounds in our hearts. He promises to answer our cry for help (verse 15) every time we pray, and His presence will be made known. Rest in that promise today.

Reflect

*W*hat are some insecurities that you have? Where did those insecurities come from? Were they planted by what people said about you? Peel back those layers of insecurity. Rewrite Psalm 91 by replacing your name where you see fit. For example, "(Insert your name) dwells in the shelter of the Most High..." Now rewrite it again with your daughter's name in the text. How empowered do you feel after doing so?

♥ *Conversation Starters* ♥

> **What labels do you use when describing yourself? What labels have others placed over you? Are they true? Let's take those labels captive. What does God say about those labels?**

Pray

Father God, thank You for creating me, loving me, and being patient with me. When the lies speak louder than the truth, Lord, remind me of who I am in You. Help me take every negative thought captive and turn it into Your beautiful truth and promises over my life. Remind me to let go of whatever keeps me from believing that I am made perfect. When I want to think You made a mistake, breathe truth and life into the depths of my soul. Lord, I thank You for this beautiful reminder. May I stand firm in it all the days of my life? In Jesus' name, I pray. Amen.

Day 7

My Hope and Stay: Relationship with God

Behold, I'm standing at the door, knocking. If your heart is open to hear my voice and you open the door within, I will come into you and feast with you, and you will feast with me.

Revelation 3:20 TPT

I didn't have the privilege of growing up in a Christian home. However, my parents did the next best thing: Every Sunday, they dropped me off at a little community church in my hometown. There, people welcomed me with smiles and loving arms. There, in that tiny community church, I felt unconditionally loved, accepted, and valued for the first time. In that sweet little church, I experienced the love of Jesus. I will forever carry the memories of Sunday school, Vacation Bible School, and mentors breathing love and light into me.

The summer after my first year of college, I was sitting in that church next to a sweet sister in Christ whom I had gone to high school with. Though my time away at college had separated us physically, it felt as if we hadn't missed a beat now that we were back together. I had missed everything about this church—the nostalgic sense of home, familiar faces, our pastor, his sermons, and the acoustic worship led by people I knew and loved. The warm fuzzies were ever-present. The sermon was on point as usual, and I felt moved by the words our pastor shared. At the end of the sermon, there was an invitation to accept Jesus as Lord and Savior. Immediately, I felt the pull to accept the invitation to receive Jesus into my heart. My feet felt so light and moved so effortlessly, it seemed as if He were carrying me to the altar. It was surreal. My friend held my hand along the way, and I was surrounded by the very same believers who had mentored me for all those years. Tears flooded my eyes, and I immediately felt a weight lift and a new sense of freedom settle.

Sister, God desires more than anything for you to know Him and grow closer to Him. Whether or not you grew up in a Christian home, He has intentionally put people in your path to help you along your faith journey. Who might those people be? Are they God-loving friends? Sisters at church? A sweet friend at work? Or an older, wiser lady who cannot wait to share the love of Jesus with you? Whomever they might be, I want to encourage you to spend more time with them. Ask them to mentor you and help you draw nearer to God. Find people who are chasing God and run the race with them.

In a world where busy is glorified, God covets our attention and wants us to make Him a priority in our lives. It's of utmost importance for me to start my day with Him and His Word. It sets the tone for my day and equips me to handle anything thrown in my way. He meets me there in that space, filling me with Holy Spirit guidance, love, and adoration. It's there that I am reminded daily of His sovereignty, mercy, grace, and provision.

Sweet sis, I hope you can find time in your day to meet with Him, even if it is for a short period. Maybe it's in your laundry room, praying over each piece of laundry as you fold it. Or while listening to a sermon in your car as you taxi your babies around town. I encourage you, friend, to set some time aside to grab a cup of coffee, open His Word, and allow Him to breathe life into you.

Friend, we have a sweet opportunity to model what it looks like to have a relationship with our heavenly Father. When our daughters witness the beautiful friendship we have with Jesus, it will encourage them to lean in and cultivate that very same relationship with our Savior. How beautiful would it be to see your daughter love Him just as much as you do?

GO DEEPER

Revelation 3:20 says, "Behold, I'm standing at the door, knocking. If your heart is open to hear my voice and you open the door within, I will come into you and feast with you, and you will feast with me." He's knocking at our door, friend. Can you hear Him? Will you let

Him in? Jesus is pulling at our hearts. He wants to know us, love us, and provide for our every need. Let's not get lost in the busyness of our schedules. So inundated that we cannot hear God's voice and His attempts to get to know us more.

Ancient Aramaic text (Jesus's native language) is translated as, "I have been standing at the door, knocking." This verse is symbolic of an ancient Jewish wedding proposal. In Jesus' day, it was a tradition that a bridegroom (the potential groom) and his father would go to the door of the bride-to-be and knock with a betrothal cup of wine and a bride-price (the cost of her hand in marriage, whether that be money or goods). If the girl were to open the door fully, it was her way of saying yes. [1] Will you accept His invitation to be His bride? Will you say yes to Jesus? When He knocks, and we submit to His love, that is where our relationship with Him begins.

God loves us so much that He desires a relationship with us. Yes, us. Zephaniah 3:17 states, He is with us always, an ever-present help. His love is so sacrificial that He sent His Son to die on the cross for us. Not only does He love us, but He also rejoices over us. I picture a proud Father, His arms crossed, face smiling ear to ear, delighted at the creation He has made. Run to Him with open arms. There's no love like the love of our Father.

---

1 Taken from "The Passion Translation" footnote Revelation 3:20

Reflect

*W*here do you struggle most in your faith? What keeps you from believing that God loves you and that His plans for your life are intentional and purposeful? Ask God to take any areas of unbelief and replace them with expectant faith.

♥ *Conversation Starters* ♥

What can you do to help grow your relationship with God? What can I do to help encourage you to spend more time with God? What can we do as a family? Who are some God-girls in your life—friends who encourage you along on your faith journey?

Pray

Father God, I want to rest in Your peace more than anything else. When my anxious heart strays, Lord, bring me back to You. Remind me that I am fully loved and known by You. You have numbered my days, and You know my path. Help me keep my path straight, and my eyes fixed on You. Lead me to rest in Your faithfulness. Help me find pockets of time when I can sit at Your feet. Lord, I desire a friendship with You. I want to know You more. I love You, God. In Jesus' name, I pray. Amen.

Day 8

God Girls: Finding Godly Influences

As iron sharpens iron, so one person sharpens another.

Proverbs 27:17 NIV

My tween and teen years were some of the most challenging years of my life, and one of the hardest things about those years was finding a group of friends who would love and accept me. I so longed for friends that I sometimes allowed others to entice me to be someone I was not. Girls came into my life who expected me to obsess over my body, dress in the best brands, and spend hours primping in the mirror. Trying to fit in with those girls also caused me to stray from my moral compass, from what I knew in my heart was right.

Sweet friend, I don't know about you, but I've realized that I don't have the time or space for toxic people as I get older. Instead, it's imperative to fill my life with people who lift me up, draw me nearer to God, and encourage me to walk obediently in faith. If only I had realized that sooner, oh the trials I would have avoided. Can you relate? While we can't change our past mistakes, we can equip our girls to weed out the bad influences and hold on to those who encourage them to grow closer to God.

Girls might come into our daughters' lives and entice them to stray from who they truly are. They may encourage them to be the mean girl, drink, vape, do drugs, have sex, or cross boundaries they wouldn't otherwise entertain. Being a part of the popular group comes with temptations to behave in ways that aren't worthy of who God has called them to be. It will be a natural impulse for them to want to fit in. But

55

our sweet girls are set apart. When they stand on that promise, they won't accept anything but God's will for their life. When they stand in that truth, they allow God to show them who their friends really are.

Let's equip our girls to find God girls—those girls who love them where they are, unconditionally, without pause. They won't require them to be anything other than themselves because they love and respect the person God has made. God girls will cheer them on when they succeed and pick them up when they fail. They don't compare or have animosity towards them because they are confident in who they are. Let's help them find girls who are chasing after Jesus even faster than they are and encourage our girls to run the race with them.

God has these perfect friendships aligned for us and our daughters. It may take some time to figure out just who those girls are, but I promise you, friend, they are there, waiting for your arrival. Don't lose heart. Stand strong and firm for you and your daughter. Refuse to allow anyone in your life who doesn't see the both of you as the perfect masterpieces God has created. When these are the stipulations you set over your friendships, God will be sure to move. His ways are purposeful. He has your back.

GO DEEPER

Iron sharpens iron through a process of friction. For a blacksmith to sharpen a piece of iron, it requires molding and shaping, sparks, and refinement. We can relate this verse to our relationships. God uses people in our lives to refine, renew, and prune us. In those godly friendships, we are encouraged, strengthened, and challenged. Sometimes those challenges cause friction but in a good, healthy, constructive criticism sort of way. We shouldn't feel discouraged by these interactions, but we should feel emboldened and empowered to find deeper connections with God.

Proverbs 27:17 challenges us to surround ourselves with people who will help us become better humans. It is said that you are the average of the five people you spend the most time with. Who are those people? Who are the women who are strong and confident? Who are the ones who aren't afraid to cheer on others because they are ridiculously secure in who they are? Are there women in your life that equip you to find deeper relations with God? Lean in and ask God to reveal the women around you who will encourage and inspire you to be the absolute best

Jesus follower you can be.

Sister, our daughters are surrounded by the people we keep in our lives. They witness our interactions with other women, and they will follow suit. When we are intentional about who we hold in our circle, we model that for our girls. When there is no room for toxicity in our relationships, our girls will create the same boundaries for themselves.

Reflect

As women, we build walls and keep to ourselves. It's difficult to trust and let people in. However, God never meant for you to navigate this "mommin'" thing on your own. What walls have you built? Do you have godly friends? If so, who are they? Where in your circle is there room for growth? Who can you invite in? Schedule a coffee date with a fellow sister in Christ whom you find inspiring.

♥ Conversation Starters ♥

Are you friends with girls who have a God-breathed confidence about them? Ones who will challenge you to follow Jesus daily. Is there a girl who radiates God's light? Who is she? How can you get to know her better?

Pray

Father God, I thank You for the women You have put in my path and those You are about to invite into my life. I know You are the God of provision. You will provide friends who will draw me closer to You, and You will bring other sisters in Christ alongside me. You are an all-knowing, all-loving God, and I know You are in the details of my friend circle. I thank You that You care about the women who will make me a better version of myself. Help me to seek the women who will sharpen me like iron. When I encounter those women, help me recognize that You have placed them in my life for such a time as this. Give me eyes to see the girls in my daughter's life. Help me nurture those relationships and encourage them along the way. In Jesus' name, I pray. Amen.

Day 9

Seeing Others Through the Eyes of God: Loving Difficult People

This is my commandment that you love one another as I have loved you.

John 15:12 NIV

When I was in high school, I had a classmate who was ridiculously rough around the edges. She was the type of girl who would find opportunities to pick at other girls, preying on their weaknesses. She targeted those who wouldn't fight back, girls she could visibly hurt and whose skin she could get under. Eventually, I became her target. I let her get to me, and I let her hurt me. Her words often stung, leaving me wondering if they were true. "You suck at field hockey. You're not an athlete. You never will be." Every time she spoke to me this way, tears would flow, giving her immediate gratification. I could see the feeling of accomplishment written all over her face.

The bullying continued until my friends and I visited the lake one day. I saw this girl from a distance. She was alone. When we got closer, I could see that her face, legs, back, and shoulders were sunburned. Oozing and raw, they were the worst sunburn blisters I had ever seen, and I could see that it was painful for her to speak. My friends invited her to come to sit with us. She sat down. She said she had walked to the lake from her home, over a mile away. When we asked where her mother was, she said she was in a meeting. She admitted that she was hungry and hadn't eaten since 2:00 a.m. I was so confused. Why would she be up at 2:00 a.m.? We offered our peanut butter and jelly sandwiches and chips to her. Joyfully accepting, she grabbed the sandwich and ate quickly.

At that moment, God showed me the pain this girl was experiencing. I didn't know what happened when she went home from school in the afternoon, but I knew that God was putting her in front of me to share a love that she might never experience inside the four walls of her own home. Seeing this girl through the eyes of her Creator came with the great responsibility to love her even when she was causing me pain. To love her anyway, even if she never extended love back. I decided I would love her in the hurt.

Have you been in a similar situation? Chances are, you've crossed paths with people within your community, people in your friend circle, or even people in your family. They challenge you to be the bigger person and love them right where they are. As Jesus followers, that is what we are called to do because people who are difficult to like, let alone love, could be carrying around some hefty baggage. May you have the eyes to see others around you who are hurting and that you dare to reach out—to be a source of love and acceptance when they have never felt lovable, approved, valuable, or worthy. The walls and facades they put up are usually a way to guard the wounds that have cut them so deeply. In these opportunities, we get to be the hands and feet of Jesus, all while encouraging our girls to come alongside us to do the same.

Be bold and courageous and love the unlovable. Be their rescue plan—God's rescue plan. In doing so, we can inspire our girls to be someone's hero as well.

GO DEEPER

In verse 9, Jesus commands us to remain in His love. Have you ever encountered the love of Jesus? If we take a step back, I am sure you can count a handful of times He's shown you His love, mercy, grace in the past week alone. Those moments when His plan finally made sense, or He made a way when there was no way possible, or you felt His comfort in suffering. What was that encounter like? How did you feel?

There's no love like the love of Jesus. No heartache that can be filled by anyone or anything else. It's beautiful, right?

We get to extend that very same sacrificial love for someone else. What if we lay down all the bitterness and resentment and love the most difficult of people the way God loves them? We get to be the love of Jesus in the flesh. This is the assignment we've been given above all else. God's greatest command, love God, love people.

Love others well. Yes, even them. The ones who seem downright terrible, awful, no good... especially them. We allow God to shine when we show others love instead of their deserved retaliation. When we extend forgiveness, mercy, and grace, God will reveal Himself through us. What happens when our persecutors expect hatred but receive love instead? Perhaps it will initiate a heart change in them. Our girls are watching. Let's make them proud. When we extend love when love isn't necessarily due, we open up the chance for our girls to witness mercy and grace. Which very well could encourage them to do the same.

Reflect

s there someone who has wronged you? What was the situation like? What do you know about this person? What could be going on that would cause this person to act like they did toward you? Pray for them. Ask God to soften their heart and work in and through them. Write that prayer in the space below. Is there a girl in your daughter's life who is difficult? How can you encourage your daughter to extend mercy and grace?

♥ Conversation Starters ♥

Is there a person in your life who is hard to love? How can you find an opportunity to extend love and kindness that they may not experience elsewhere? How would it feel for you to love them and accept them for who they are? How do you think it would make them feel?

_____
_____
_____
_____
_____
_____
_____
_____
_____
_____
_____
_____
_____
_____
_____
_____
_____
_____
_____
_____
_____
_____
_____
_____

Pray

Father God, help me love others and see them through Your eyes. I know you have created every person on this planet. There's not a person whom You don't love. Help me love them through their rough edges. Help me find peace in knowing that You are doing a good work in them in Your time, not mine. Give me the courage to love others even when I feel they are undeserving. In doing so, I hope that I can encourage my daughter to love those around her as you love them.
In Jesus' name, I pray. Amen.

Day 10

Strength to Stand: Peer Pressure

Do not conform to the pattern of this world but be transformed by the renewing of your mind. Then you will be able to test and approve what God's will is—his good, pleasing and perfect will.

Romans 12:2 NIV

Friend, our girls are under immense pressure, and pressure from the closest friends might seem like the most difficult to overcome. This is because that pressure comes with the temptation to believe that they will be loved and accepted if they do what others ask or expect of them. Our girls' friends might pressure them to always look influencer-worthy and social media-ready. Some other pressures might include but are not limited to having a relationship, having sex, sending nude photos, vaping, acting differently around certain people, conforming to cultural norms, bullying others, and gossiping. The list could go on.

Why do people feel the need to entice our girls to overstep these kinds of boundaries? When someone is asking them to do something that is not in line with who they are, it's because they've overstepped that very same boundary themselves. They attempt to feel better about their decisions by inviting our girls into that same unwise decision. But just because they've been invited into the sin doesn't mean our daughters have to accept that invitation.

Personally, I've learned the hard way that jeopardizing my integrity by overstepping boundaries is a costly mistake. It has caused heartache and many tears. We can help our daughters avoid this pain. When someone invites our girls to toe the line of right and wrong, let's encourage them to pray. Ask them to invite God into that space. Ask that He give our daughters the courage to remain true to who they are and who He has created them to be. It's there in that scary place of peer pressure that they can see God move in the situation. He won't lead them astray. He will lead our sweet girls, speak the words for them, and give them courage and peace that will help them overcome any pressure others might place on them.

Our daughters are not defined by what they wear, how they look, their boyfriend, how many "friends" they have on social, how many friends they have in "real life," the label on their purse, or the car they drive. Sweet sis, they are so much more. They weren't born to fit in because God created them to be "set apart." Having faith in Jesus makes them look different — holy, in fact. That word might scare them. I know it scares me. Having faith in Jesus means we set boundaries—we decide in advance what we are willing and not willing to do in this life based upon biblical standards. While it may seem weird and going against the status quo, we live faithfully the way God intended us to live.

In living this way, we inspire others to walk with God too. When we shine bright, radiate joy, and have a peace about us that just makes little sense to the outside world, we create opportunities to share God's faithfulness.

Let's encourage our daughters to stand confidently in who they are—who God has created them to be—and to be steadfast. Being popular is so overrated.

GO DEEPER

"The patterns of this world" ... I think we can all agree this world is not our home and the cultural norms that are being thrown at our girls are downright scary to navigate. God calls us to live righteous and holy. If we are going to live a set-apart life, we need to know biblical truth. When the world is leading others astray, we can stand firm on His word and His ways. We don't have to feel pressured to conform to immoral beliefs because we know the standards He has set before us.

In Romans 12:2, the apostle Paul inspires us to ignore the societal norms of this world and transform our minds in the process. The transformation of our thought processes causes us to align all thoughts with biblical truth. Culture might cause us to question and waiver, but it's never been more important to check that thought life with a biblical filter.

Our daughters' circle of influence might invite them to overstep the boundaries God has placed for them. When the world is obnoxiously loud and confusing, let's encourage our girls to live a righteous life. Holy and sound, deeply rooted in what the Bible has spoken over them. When they lay down the need to fit in and reposition their hearts and minds toward God, they will remain steadfast in their faith and won't find a need to waiver. Let's champion a generation of girls willing to fight for righteousness.

Reflect

 hat types of peer pressure might your daughter be facing? Journal a prayer over your daughter. Ask God to protect her from any temptation that might come her way. When the temptation comes, invite God to help her overcome and remain steadfast.

♥ Conversation Starters ♥

Have you ever been asked to cross a line? What boundary were you invited to cross? How did you respond? Did you feel a heart pull in either direction? This is the perfect opportunity to talk with your girl about the Holy Spirit and how He works. Explain to her that when we feel in our heart that a decision is wrong, this is the Holy Spirit guiding us. Encourage her to invite God into her decision making and ask the Holy Spirit to help her make the holy choice.

_____

_____

_____

_____

_____

_____

_____

_____

_____

_____

_____

_____

_____

_____

_____

_____

_____

_____

_____

_____

_____

_____

_____

_____

Pray

Father God, give my daughter peace in who she is and the path You wish for her to follow. Please direct her in that path, Lord. I thank You for Jesus and that He came to this earth to exemplify who we need to be. Lord, show me how we can be more like Jesus. When others pressure my daughter to grasp onto the things of this world, give her the strength to hold on to the guide rails you've placed before her.
In Jesus' name, I pray. Amen.

Day 11

God's Battle Plan: Enduring Difficult Times

For our struggle is not against flesh and blood, but against the rulers, against the authorities, against the powers of this dark world, and against the spiritual forces of evil in the heavenly realms. Therefore, put on the whole armor of God so that when the day of evil comes, you may be able to stand your ground, and after you have done everything, to stand.

Ephesians 6:12-13 NIV

God says we will experience trials of many kinds. Friend, I am sure you've experienced your fair share in your lifetime. I once heard that we could divide the battles we face into two categories: little "t" traumas and big "T" traumas. Let me explain. Big "T" traumas are events such as losing a child or enduring a life-threatening experience, such as almost dying in a car accident. A little "t" trauma is an event that isn't necessarily life-threatening but is still difficult to overcome. Such little "t" traumas might include emotional abuse, losing a friendship, losing a job, etc.

As a girl, I had my fair share of both types of trauma. I was considered poor, lowly, and among the least of these. Easily overlooked and grossly underestimated, many believed I wouldn't amount to anything in this life. They weren't afraid to share those expectations. However, in the trials and battles, I found fuel to prove the naysayers wrong. I wasn't about to let others put limitations on me.

Perhaps one of the most difficult traumas you will face in your life are the trials your children encounter. They may technically fall under the little "t" traumas, but they feel like a big "T" trauma to a mama's heart. The mama bear instinct is real, and I have to think that God put it there for a reason. We just want to protect our little cubs. At times it might seem that the world is coming at them, and you might feel completely helpless and out of control.

I'm writing this book in the middle of a pandemic. The toll it has taken on one of my children has been astronomical. Isolation is a real thing. I cannot tell you the complete story because it is not my story to tell. I can, however, share what it was like from my perspective.

This past year has taken my child to dark places. Isn't it just like the enemy to meet a child in their bedroom while enduring a dark, scary, uncertain time? Feeding that child with lies and schemes. My husband and I felt helpless. We lost sleep, appetite, and gained a grey hair or two. I felt like a newborn mother again, waking up in the middle of the night, tiptoeing to my child's bedroom, leaning over their chest, watching for the rise and fall of their lungs to make sure they were breathing and still alive. We wanted so badly to make the hurt and pain go away. There were times when I just wanted to fast forward into my child's adulthood to see them prosperous and whole again.

We fasted, set the alarm on our phones to pray each day at noon, wrote verses and post-it notes of scripture, and placed them under their mattress. God put women in my life who spoke of my child's restoration. They pointed me to scripture and the promise that one day this child would be healed and set free from the bondage that held them captive. One day God reminded me that He loved this child more than I ever could. Seems unfathomable, right, mama? That He had created them, He had a plan for them, a plan to prosper and not to harm them. It was in that whisper that God had called me to let go and to surrender control to Him. That He too felt my burden, helplessness, and pain and what the enemy meant for harm, He promised to turn to good.

Letting go and letting God is not a simple task. Raising these babies in the way they should go is a mission field, my friend. Living a righteous life in today's world has proven extremely difficult. However, we can stand confident that God is in it all, and He promises victory over the hearts and minds of our children. God is within them. They cannot fail. Hold on to His promises, Love.

The way we navigate these traumas matters to God. When circumstances arise, we have the power to put on God's armor. He's in our battles. Nothing we face will ever surprise God because He is all-knowing. Before you were born, God knew what traumas you would have to overcome.

Some days your suffering will seem downright unfair and unjust, but in that hurt, pain, and sadness, God will show up, making you stronger than you have ever been before. One day you will look back and laugh in the face of those trials because it made you the strongest, most faith-filled, God warrior you have ever known. There is light at the end of every trial, and His name is Jesus. Fix your eyes on Him, sister. Your battle is already won if you give it to Him. Bless and release, give your battles to Him, and you will see victory.

GO DEEPER

The Bible states that we will face trials of many kinds (James 1:2), but it's in our circumstances that we have an opportunity to surrender our battles to the One who promises to see us through. In these verses from Ephesians, Paul lays out a battle plan for us. But first, he reminds us that the attacks and trials we face in this life aren't from flesh and blood but from the enemy himself. I don't know about you, but I find mercy and grace for my persecutors when I realize they are dealing with their own demons. Satan uses people just like God uses people. They don't know what they don't know. Their actions and words are used for Satan's plan, not God's. That prompts me to pray for them and see them for who they are—hurting human beings.

For further encouragement, go to Matthew 16:18 when Jesus tells Peter, "On this rock I will build my church, and the gates of Hades will not overcome it." The church, that's us, sweet friend. Jesus says we will not be overcome by the evil plans of the enemy. I hope that brings you peace today.

In verse 13, Paul tells us to put on the whole armor of God and stand confident that He is battling for you. That armor includes truth, righteousness, the gospel of peace, faith, salvation, and the Word of God. You can find rest in Jesus because, girl, He is already in the battle. You can confidently claim victory in His wonderful name. That's powerful.

Reflect

*H*ave you recently dealt with a disappointment or an attack? If so, what was it? How can God's battle plan listed in Ephesians 6:12-17 help you cope with the situation differently? How does knowing that God is in your battles equip you to release the outcome in your circumstances?

♥ Conversation Starters ♥

> Do you know that God is present in every battle you face? How does that make you feel? What battles have you overcome? Can you see how God worked in those battles if you look back? How did He show you, His presence?

Pray

Father God, I know my daughter, and I will face trials of many kinds in this life. No matter what we face, Lord, I know You are on our side. If You are for us, who can stand against? Help me extend mercy and grace to our persecutors and remind me that my battle isn't against them but against a spiritual enemy attacking us. In my weakness, give me the strength to pray for those who hurt my girl and me. When we are in the depths of our battles, Lord, help me turn my eyes to You and stand confident that the victory is already won. In Jesus' name, I pray. Amen.

Day 12

Loving God's Creation: Kindness

Put on then, as God's chosen ones, holy and beloved, compassionate hearts, kindness, humility, meekness, and patience.

Colossians 3:12 NIV

There's a lot of division in our world today. Walls have been built between race and gender. It's almost as if we walk in our world today not knowing how to act, behave, or how to feel. So many assumptions are put on people. Eye contact is hard. We've been living under masks for 18 months. We could hide our thoughts and emotions behind that mask. As Christians, God calls us to walk differently. To see each human as His purposeful creation. We can change the trajectory of cultural norms by just being kind.

God calls us to be the light of the world, and I can't think of a better way to express that light than being kind and loving. As mothers, we get to model what that looks like for our daughters. We can demonstrate kindness by looking for opportunities to randomly love others when it isn't expected. Doing so can be as simple as making eye contact, smiling warmly, saying "Good to see you today," or giving a hug when you sense someone needs one.

Kindness is so important to God that the apostle Paul includes it in his list of fruits of the Spirit found in Galatians 5:22-23. In a world where many people are hurting, you have an abundance of opportunities to share God's love and kindness.

Why is kindness called a fruit? The word fruit doesn't mean food that we eat but means the goodness we produce due to the Holy Spirit living in our hearts. When we follow the little God whispers from the

Holy Spirit, we will produce this kind of "spiritual fruit." (If you're not sure what the Holy Spirit's guidance feels like, consider this question: Have you ever heard a soft whisper or felt a heart pull that tells you to go talk to someone, compliment someone, or extend love in one way or another? That, my friend, is the Holy Spirit working in you.) The things those whispers prompt us to do may seem weird and out of sorts. Still, I promise, if you follow through with them, you will be blessed in your obedience, producing love and joy, peace, and kindness—God's holy work inside of you. What a blessing it will be when our daughters come alongside us and develop that same sense of Holy Spirit direction and become the ambassadors of kindness God has called them to be.

As Christians, our ultimate goal is to love like Jesus every day. We have to get to know Him and learn by His example to love like Him. Here in this devotional, you are learning about Jesus daily. That kind of dedication will breathe life and love into your heart and mind and cause you and your sweet girl to love boldly on His behalf. Together, let's throw kindness around like confetti!

GO DEEPER

The Passion Translation of Colossians 4:12 states that we are to "Robe yourself with the virtues of God, since you have been divinely chosen to be holy." Compassion, kindness, humility, gentleness, and patience are relational attributes. Virtues of God that we are to carry out daily. We shouldn't take this assignment lightly. He was purposeful when He called us into His kingdom. To be shepherds of His flock and to love them well.

People know we are Christians, and they are very attentive to our actions. Maya Angelou once said, "I've learned that people will forget what you said, people will forget what you did, but people will never forget how you made them feel." Let's be the reason someone feels the love of Jesus today.

You are chosen, holy, and loved. Because God loved you so much that He sent His Son to die for you, He asks that you extend that very same agape love (unconditional love from God) to all those around you. We share that love when we show kindness and are humble. That means we aren't walking around thinking we are better than anyone else, but instead, we see others as Jesus sees them: as someone to love.

Reflect

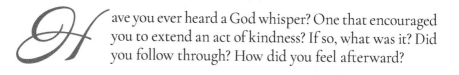 ave you ever heard a God whisper? One that encouraged you to extend an act of kindness? If so, what was it? Did you follow through? How did you feel afterward?

♥ *Conversations with Your Girl*
♥

What are some ways that we as a family can love and show kindness to those around us? Is there another family we can serve? Could we bake cookies for an elderly neighbor? Or send handwritten letters to someone we love and appreciate? Choose one and act on it.

Pray

Father God, thank You that You loved me so much that You sent Your Son to die for me. Thank You for challenging me to love others as You love me. Empower me daily to act on that Holy Spirit guidance to show Your love, Lord. Help me see opportunities to extend a helping hand where You see fit. I seek nothing in return but find joy in being Your hands and feet here on earth. When I do these things in Your name and for Your glory, my daughter will be a witness to the light you shine within me. In Jesus' name, I pray. Amen.

Day 13

Dealing with the Sour Puss: Attitudes

*Do all things without grumbling or questioning, that you may
be blameless and innocent, children of God without blemish in
the midst of a crooked and twisted generation, among whom you
shine as lights in the world.*

Philippians 2:14-15 NIV

If I could go back and redo all those times my mama asked me to wash
the dishes, I would. Instead of storming off and rolling my eyes—or,
when I did them, washing them haphazardly—I would show respect
by taking pride in my work and honoring my parents by making sure
every plate, cup, and pan were sparkly clean. I would choose to have a
good attitude and show love through my obedience because, now that
I'm a mama, I know how difficult it is to deal with attitudes in our
girls. Have you ever left an argument with your daughter wondering
how it went so poorly so quickly? Nothing gets under my skin like
a good eye roll, the cold shoulder, grumbling under the breath, or
disregarding what is said. But it's so easy to respond to such behavior
with my own eye roll or sarcastic comment.

But what if we met the attitude and poor heart posture with love,
grace, mercy, and kindness? That will for sure take them off their guard.
The way we respond to the attitude will determine the trajectory of the
behavior. We can meet them right where they are. In the hurt, pain,
and sadness projecting in poor behavior, we can show them we love
them. I know it's easier said than done, but we get to equip them to
react differently next time by showing them we won't go toe to toe with
them and their attitude.

Our girls are the change we want to see in the world, our homes, the playing field, and our classrooms simply by adjusting their attitude and heart posture. And we are the ones who get to help them decide what vibe they want to carry. We are the ones who get to help them decide whether they want to be known for being courteous, kind, and genuinely grateful or whether they will be notorious for their stink face. We get to help them find opportunities to see the good in all situations regardless of what comes their way.

As followers of Jesus, we know that there will be temptations to fall into stinkin' thinking, which turns into stinkin' attitudes. But you must resist any thoughts that hold you in a negative headspace. As Philippians 4:8 says, "Whatever is true, whatever is noble, whatever is right, whatever is pure, whatever is lovely, whatever is admirable—if anything is excellent or praiseworthy—think about such things." Remember, how you behave is often how your daughter will behave.

GO DEEPER:

Let's visit The Passion Translation's version of these verses. "Live a cheerful life, without complaining or division among ourselves. For then you will be seen as innocent, faultless, and pure children of God, even though you live in a brutal and perverse culture. For you will appear among them as shining lights in the universe, holding out the words of eternal life."

Philippians 2:14-16

The opposite of a bad attitude is a cheerful heart. We get to choose our heart posture. We cannot control our situations or circumstances, but we can control how we react and see the problem. When circumstances arise that test us, let's choose a position of humility. Laying down self-righteousness, bitterness, and complaint and pray. Ask God to show us how He sees the situation and how we should aid in a positive outcome.

We have a great responsibility as believers to walk differently than others. Instead of grumbling and complaining, we are called to shine Jesus' light for all to see. In Philippians 2:14-15, Paul, our encourager, challenges us to humble ourselves and our girls and carry a sense of peace with us. When we walk in peace and joy, others will question where our hope comes from. Our positivity becomes contagious, shining a bright light for all to see.

Reflect

*T*ake your negative thoughts captive. Set a timer for one hour. During that hour, I want you to journal any negative thought patterns. After that hour, take 10-15 minutes to turn that negativity into something positive and praiseworthy.

♥ Conversation Starters ♥

How can you share joy today? When the stinkin' thinkin' rears its ugly head, how can you reposition your heart to a place of gratitude, love, and light? Have you had overwhelming negative thoughts in a current situation in your life? How did you react? Do you think your attitude poorly affected someone else? If so, could you reach out to that someone and apologize for your poor attitude and ask for forgiveness?

Pray

Father God, I thank You that You convict us when our attitudes don't align with who You want us to be. Help me see where we can change our heart posture and turn it into light. Help us to shine that light in the dark places in our lives. Lord, surround us with fellow light-bearers so our light may magnify and glorify You. Thank You, Lord, for loving us where we are and encouraging us to be better versions of ourselves today and all our tomorrows.
In Jesus' name, I pray. Amen.

Day 14

Check Yourself Before You Wreck Yourself: Making Good Choices

Flee the evil desires of youth and pursue righteousness, faith, love, and peace, along with those who call on the Lord out of a pure heart.

2 Timothy 2:22 NIV

It can be hard for our children to decipher what to believe, how to live, and what boundaries to set in a noisy and confusing world. Social media influences, such as TikTok, Snapchat, YouTube, and Google, will try to slowly persuade them to believe things that aren't morally right in the eyes of God. If we're not careful, soon societal norms become their new norm.

Our daughters may also have friends who encourage them to cross boundaries they weren't meant to cross. They may be invited to parties or pressured to drink, smoke, and do drugs. What will they do if someone insists they smoke weed? What if a boyfriend tries to persuade them to go to his bedroom and expects something physical from them? We, as moms, can help them decide how they will respond to such pressures before they come. How? By praying for our daughters, encouraging them to take a stand and ask themselves if their choices will honor God or force them to sin against Him, and equipping them with God's truths and guidance before they are in situations that make them feel uncomfortable, squirmy, and afraid to say no.

We can also equip our daughters to respond in righteousness by reminding them that if something feels wrong in their hearts, listen to that still small voice. We can help them recognize that the little whisper saying, "Don't do it," is the Holy Spirit warning them that they are about to cross a line. God put that Holy Spirit's guidance in our daughters' hearts to help lead, guide, and direct them in this confusing life. The Holy Spirit is God living within them. We can help them stand firm in what they know is true, noble, kind, and praiseworthy and build their moral compass on the Rock, the God of all creation Who is consistently moral and just.

The world is full of pressures of many kinds. Pressures to fit in, pressures to feel accepted, pressures to be seen. Your daughter is already all those things in the eyes of God. She doesn't need to cross any lines to feel accepted because she is already fully loved and known by her loving Creator.

GO DEEPER

The Merriam Dictionary defines righteousness as "acting with divine or moral law: free from guilt or sin." [2] We can't expect our girls to be perfect. Jesus was the only one who could attain such goals. However, we can encourage them to live according to the Spirit living within them. I love how The Passion Translation says, "Run as fast as you can from all the ambitions and lusts of youth, and chase after all that is pure."

The enemy, Satan, seeks to steal, kill, and destroy. He wants nothing more than to persuade us to live a life outside of God's will. Don't fall into his lies. Not for even a millisecond. The enemy knows our daughters' weaknesses, and he will prey on them, trying to find an opportunity to weasel his way into her life. Like a lion, Satan attacks us in our most vulnerable spaces (1 Peter 5:8).

"So then, surrender to God. Stand up to the devil and resist him, and he will flee in agony" James 4:7 TPT. The enemy will flee in agony because of the God who stands with us and for us. I love how this verse gives us encouragement and hope in our battles against Satan. Let's empower our girls to submit themselves to God: all of them, all for Him. They don't need to cross lines and boundaries to fit in or please others—they already have that approval in the eyes of their heavenly Father.

---

2 https://www.mirriam-webster.com/dictionary/righteousness

Reflect

*H*as there ever been a time where you felt the Holy Spirit's direction in a decision? What was that situation like? Did you feel Satan's heart pull in the opposite direction of God's still voice? What choice did you make? How did your heart feel afterward? Our girls are experiencing the same inner turmoil. How can you equip her to handle these tough decisions that she will have to make?

Make a list of boundaries you do not want your girl to cross. That list might include having sex, vaping, drinking alcohol, sexual immorality, or using drugs. Discuss those boundaries with your girl.

♥ Conversation Starters ♥

It's time to have the tough conversations. You can do hard things, sweet friend. These aren't easy discussions to have, but I promise you it's easier to have them now than later. It can be as simple as telling them, "I am here if you ever need me." Planting a seed by letting her know that she is invited to an open line of communication, and she can come to you at any time. You promise to not judge or lecture. Keep the door open for discussion. Don't ever close it because chances are if you react, explode, place judgment and shame, or even show them you are too busy, the door will never be opened again.

Pray

Dear Father God, I thank You for Your Holy Spirit's guidance. What would we do without You, Lord? Thank You for living inside of us and helping us navigate this scary life. Lord, I know that the enemy prowls in the dark spaces of our lives. Come and bring light to those places and lead, guide, and light our paths. Empower my daughter to stand against the enemy when he's seeking to take her to dark places. Show her Your ways and remind her that the enemy will flee when she submits to You. Thank You for never leaving her or forsaking her. In Jesus' name, I pray. Amen.

Day 15

Her Approval Has Been Won: Rejection

He was despised and rejected by humanity, a man of suffering and familiar with pain. Like one from whom people hide their faces, he was despised, and we held him in low esteem.

Isaiah 53:3 NIV

I was well into my 40s before I realized that my constant need to strive for more was a behavior that had grown from a deep seed of rejection. Having faced rejection after rejection in childhood and adulthood, I worked tirelessly to be seen, loved, worthy, heard, and approved. It wasn't until I peeled back the layers of all the past hurts and rejections and uprooted those weeds that I allowed God to meet me in that pain. It was there that He invited me to uproot the orphan spirit that I had embraced for so long. It was there that He reminded me that He adopted me into His royal priesthood the moment He formed me in my mother's womb. In this pruning, I began to cultivate an identity solely focused on Him. As I did that, I began to experience true acceptance.

In today's world, our daughters may face the same feelings of rejection I did while growing up—the same feelings of rejection you may have encountered. Social media is like rejection on steroids. Our girls don't even have to be told they don't belong. They just sense it. All they have to do is open an app to see that they were not invited, not worthy of being involved, and not seen. Perhaps our daughters find that their friends had a party they didn't know about. Or they didn't get the "likes" they hoped to get on their latest post. Or even worse, someone dared to pick at their flaws publicly for the world to see, only highlighting what they already felt self-conscious about.

Take heart, friend. We can remind our sweet girls that even Jesus was despised and rejected. He came to save the world, yet He was the most rejected person in all of humanity. He loved the lowly and the weak and came so that we would experience God in the flesh. Though He was blameless, those around Him couldn't see His value. He didn't live up to their expectations of who they thought He should be.

We know all too well that girls can be mean. This may be the most difficult season for our girls to find where they belong. Middle school and high school are rough on everyone. Let's inspire them to remain steadfast. Like Jesus, rejection can't hurt them when they sit confidently in God's acceptance and approval.

GO DEEPER

The prophet Isaiah wrote the Old Testament book of Isaiah 700 years before the birth of Jesus. He predicted that Jesus would be rejected. Not only rejected but despised. God's chosen people (Israel), the very same people Jesus came to save, refused to accept Him. As we discussed earlier, the Jews expected the Messiah to be a warrior king like David. But Jesus came humbly, loving sinners, crossing lines, and bringing down barriers.

In Matthew 21:42 TPT, "Jesus said to them, 'Haven't you ever read the Scripture that says: The very stone the builder rejected as flawed has now become the most important cornerstone.' This was the Lord's plan, isn't it marvelous to behold?" God knew in advance that the Jewish people would reject Jesus. He wasn't at all who they expected him to be. They overlooked Him, criticized him, and refused to believe He was the Messiah. It was their loss; they missed out.

Because we are disciples of Christ and refuse to align with the things of this world, there's a good chance we will be rejected as well. In fact, Jesus says we can expect to be persecuted. "Just remember, when the unbelieving world hates you, they first hated me. If you were to give your allegiance to this world, they would love and welcome you as one of their own. But because you won't align yourself with the world's values, they will hate you. I have chosen you and taken you out of the world to be mine." John 15:18-19 TPT The pressure is off, sweet sis. We don't have to measure up to the patterns of this world. We are His. Fully known, loved, and accepted just as we are.

Reflect

Have past rejections caused you pain? What are those rejections? Write them out. Have you taken those rejections to God? Laid them at His feet? Write a prayer surrendering the rejection to God once and for all. Ask Him to uproot any pain that has been caused by those who have rejected the person God has created you to be.

Has your daughter been rejected? What were those circumstances? Write out a prayer for her as well. Ask that God give her the courage to surrender those past hurts to Him and invite Him to meet her in that pain.

♥ *Conversation Starters* ♥

Have you ever felt rejected? If so, what was the situation like? Does that rejection make you feel unworthy? Does that pain still hurt? Jesus was rejected as well. He wasn't the man that the Jewish leaders expected. How does that bring you comfort? After talking with your girl, read the prayer you wrote for her aloud to her.

Pray

Father God, thank You for sending Your Son so that He may be an encouragement to us. Lord, I know Jesus was rejected, mocked, and made fun of. Help us find strength in His trials and inspiration to overcome our own suffering. I pray for a hedge of protection over my daughter against the feelings of rejection. Guard her heart and mind when others attempt to make her feel "less than" and unworthy. Give her courage to stand in Your favor and approval all the days of her life.
In Jesus' name, I pray. Amen.

Day 16

You've Got a Friend in Me: Friendship Loss

The righteous cry out, and the Lord hears them;
he delivers them from all their troubles.
The Lord is close to the brokenhearted
and saves those who are crushed in spirit.
The righteous person may have many troubles,
but the Lord delivers him from them all.

Psalm 34:17-19 NIV

I can remember like it was yesterday. There was a person I trusted with my deepest secrets. Then one day, out of nowhere, she turned on me. The betrayal cut deep within my heart. It left me confused, wondering where things had gone wrong. She was my person. We did everything together. I thought she would be my best friend forever. Instead, she said hurtful things and caused pain that haunts me to this day.

Broken, lonely, and baffled at the sudden loss of someone who occupied a large space within my heart, I found myself questioning my identity. *Am I the monster she said I am?* I wondered. Not only was there pain from the fallout, but there was also fear of ever allowing someone to get that close to me again. It took months for me to process the hurt, but in the end, I realized that I came out stronger because of it. In fact, I thank God for all that I endured because it made me the person I am today: strong in my faith and able to rely solely on God to fulfill me. He showed up in big ways during that time, picking up the pieces, mending the brokenness, and revealing His plans for me. Plans that were bigger than I could ever imagine. I was happy again, all because of letting go and relying on Him.

There's a good chance that our daughters will face the very same scenario in their teenage years. Friends they saw as forever sisters might change, disappoint them, and perhaps even disown them. Losing a friend can be more difficult than a loss of a boyfriend. We become our daughters' source of God's encouragement, redirection, and guidance in the brokenness that follows such a loss.

Friends may come and go. That doesn't make it easy to process—there's no loss like the loss of a friend. It may feel like the end of the world to our girls. The betrayal of someone they let in and invested their heart and soul into is heartbreaking. However, I do have good news. God will meet them right there in the middle of their suffering. Just when they think they can't possibly move on, He shows up. Each day, the next step becomes easier, His light shining a little brighter. One day they will look back and see that His plan was so perfect all along.

GO DEEPER

"The righteous cry out, and the Lord hears them"

Psalm 34:17.

Does your heart physically feel burdened when your child is hurting? Like there's a sudden pang or zap in your heart when your baby is injured. I picture the same happening when God sees our pain. His heart hurts for us. When we cry out for our children, He hears us. Our cries do not fall on deaf ears. God invites us to audibly cry out and pour out our hearts. It's in that pain and suffering that God meets us right there in that moment.

No matter what we might be going through, God is there, an ever-present help in time of need. Let's encourage our girls to lay down the hurt. Be open, honest, vulnerable, and authentic with God. Tell Him how they feel. He hears the cries of our hearts. When we open up and say what we feel, we give Him permission to mend the brokenness and make us whole again.

Philippians 4:19 TPT states, "I am convinced that my God will fully satisfy every need you have, for I have seen the abundant riches of glory revealed to me through Jesus Christ!" Satisfy. That word. Does it bring you peace? God promises to satisfy the desires of our hearts. While others might let us down, God is the only place we can turn to, to find lasting, unwavering, unshakeable satisfaction. I pray our girls can bask in the glory of that satisfaction.

Reflect

*H*ave you ever lost a close friend? Were you left confused? Betrayed? Was it difficult to trust again? How has God worked in your friendships in the past? Did He provide a new friend? Have confidence that He will provide again.

♥ Conversation Starters ♥

Have you lost a friend? What pain did that cause? How did God show up in that situation? Is there any remaining pain you are holding onto with regard to the hurt? How can I pray for you in that brokenness? Pray together with your girl.

Pray

Father God, I know within my heart of hearts that You have ordained our steps right down to every last detail. I know that You have a good and perfect plan for us. You are in even the smallest of details. Even something as small as our friendships. Lord, surround my girl and me with God girls who chase You faster than us. Women who celebrate our family and lift us up when we are down. Help us find girls who glorify You. In Jesus' name, I pray. Amen.

Day 17

Made Perfect: Body Image

The Lord does not look at the things people look at. People look at the outward appearance, but the Lord looks at the heart.

1 Samuel 16:7b NIV

Skinny is not a word that is used to describe me. Being one-quarter Finnish, I inherited a Viking build: solid and muscular with a stocky frame. As I grew up, I learned that this body type was not considered ideal. Driven by the desire to achieve the kind of appearance the world valued and by the need for love and acceptance from others, I pursued a myriad of diets, one after another. I would lose 20 pounds only to gain 30, always searching for the next fad diet to reach my goals. It didn't matter what size I got; even the most petite sizes were never enough. I wanted more. I was never content with my weight and always sought the next best fix. My identity eventually morphed into the number on the scale. I weighed myself each morning, even going as far as bringing the scale with me on overnight trips.

I thought I'd find happiness in my clothing size, in the number on the scale, and in validation from others. Truth is, those were empty ambitions that left me feeling drained. The madness continued until God convicted me. That still small voice asked me to realign my priorities.

God doesn't want us women to idolize skinny. Every moment we spend hating the image we see in the mirror or resenting our flaws hurts His heart. When we decide we don't like the body we are in, we are basically telling God that He made a mistake in creating us. God loves us so much. When He looks at us, He sees perfection. Picture a proud Father looking down at His precious daughter with pride and adoration, a sweet little smile on His face that says, "You are the apple of my eye." That's how God sees us. He created you. He purposefully made you who you are, right down to every last detail.

If we struggle with body image, we subconsciously invite our girls to do the same. Maybe they see us working out tirelessly, beating our bodies into submission. Or they witness us stepping on the scale each morning and then stepping off with a look of disappointment yet again. Or they observe us obsessing over every morsel of food we put in our mouths, skipping the trip to the ice cream store, or declining the slice of cake at their birthday party. We are role models for our daughters, and when we engage in these behaviors, they will likely imitate us. When we decide that our bodies aren't good enough, we allow our daughters to witness their mothers being discontent with the creation God has made. However, when we accept our body as God's temple and treat it as such, we are better able to be at peace in our own skin.

Our daughters face an overwhelming number of images that portray bodily perfection. Those images compete for their attention and invite them to believe that they have to fit into worldly standards. The good news is we don't have to allow our daughters to fit the mold of cultural body norms. Through our own body acceptance, we can encourage our girls to remain confident in the beautiful body God made for them.

GO DEEPER

1 Samuel 16:7b in context is actually talking about young David. God sent Samuel to anoint David as Saul's successor. In the eyes of the world, David was unfit. He was between the ages of 10-15. That's the age of our girls. David was young in the eyes of the world, but in the eyes of God, he was precisely the man for the job. Why? His heart. God was looking for a man after His own heart.

The moment you receive Jesus as your Lord and Savior is when the Holy Spirit takes residence within you. I Corinthians 6:19-20 NIV, "Do you not know that your bodies are temples of the Holy Spirit, who is in you, whom you have received from God? You are not your own; you were bought at a price. Therefore, honor God with your bodies." Christ died for the body you live in. He considered you that precious to Him. He didn't ask you to change the way you look, manipulate your body to submit to cultural standards or strive to be someone other than the perfect creation He made. No, He saw you just as you are, and He said it is good.

The world will judge us on our outward appearance. We will even get caught up in judging ourselves. However, God sees the beauty and splendor of our hearts, and He calls it good. Not just good—more precious than rubies, a beautiful masterpiece, perfectly constructed by our mighty God.

Reflect

*A*re you accepting of your own body? If not, take some time today to ask God to reveal areas of striving for a better body. Ask Him to replace the striving with His love and acceptance of who you are and the body He has created for you. Does your girl compare her body to those around her? What steps can you take to promote a body-positive environment at home?

♥ Conversation Starters ♥

If you've struggled with your body image and your daughter has witnessed some of the strivings, this might be a good time to confess that to her. Lead an open conversation about this topic. It might sound like, "Hey sis, I know you've seen me dieting and exercising a lot. I used to think that I had to work really hard to love my body, but God revealed to me recently that I am already loved." After sharing your experience, create a list of body-positive, scripture-based affirmations together.

Here are some verses to get you started:

- For we are God's handiwork, created in Christ Jesus to do good works, which God prepared in advance for us to do. Ephesians 2:10 NIV

- Do you not know that your bodies are temples of the Holy Spirit, who is in you, whom you have received from God? 1 Corinthians 6:19 NIV

- So, God created mankind in his own image, in the image of God, he created them; male and female, he created them. Genesis 1:27 NIV

- I praise you because I am fearfully and wonderfully made; your works are wonderful; I know that full well. Psalm 139:14 NIV

- Let's just be what we were made to be, without enviously or pridefully comparing ourselves with each other or trying to be something we aren't. Romans 12:6 MSG

- I sought the Lord, and he answered me;

- he delivered me from all my fears.

Those who look to him are radiant; their faces are never covered with shame.

Psalm 34:4-5 NIV

Pray

Father God, thank You for loving me from the inside out. Lord, forgive me when I look at the person You have created and pick her apart. Reveal the influences in my life that keep me from resting in Your peace. Help me find confidence in every square inch of the beautiful body You made. When my mind begins to compare or insult Your creation, prompt me to take that thought captive and renew my mind with Your truths. Equip me to raise my daughter in full belief that she is Your masterpiece, lacking nothing. Breathe love and acceptance into her being, Lord. Help her to remain confident in the beautiful creation. You have made.
In Jesus' name, I pray. Amen.

Day 18

I Will Not Allow My Daughter to be the Victim: Bullying

43 "You have heard that it was said, 'Love your neighbor and hate your enemy.' 44 But I tell you, love your enemies and pray for those who persecute you, 45 that you may be children of your Father in heaven. He causes his sun to rise on the evil and the good and sends rain on the righteous and the unrighteous. 46 If you love those who love you, what reward will you get? Are not even the tax collectors doing that? 47 And if you greet only your own people, what are you doing more than others? Do not even pagans do that? 48 Be perfect, therefore, as your heavenly Father is perfect.

Matthew 5:43-48 NIV

One day when I was in sixth grade, I walked into the school bathroom, and a flash of white fabric dangling from the top of one stall caught my eye. Upon closer inspection, I was horrified to discover that it was a bra with a post-it note attached to it that said, "Trudy's bra." Along with the post-it note, there was a Kleenex dangling from the bra. As I quickly left the bathroom, red-faced and with tears filling my eyes, several girls stood huddled outside the bathroom doors, giggling and pointing.

Due to awkward growth patterns in my tween years, I developed way ahead of the other girls in my class. And to my dismay, my development became a huge source of teasing. Accusations of stuffing my bra (hence the Kleenex attached to the bra in the bathroom) was a long-standing joke among the 6th-grade class. So much so the boys joined in on the fun, calling me "Twin Peaks" at every opportunity they could find.

My deepest longing was to be loved, appreciated, and accepted. Still, my classmates' endless taunting left me feeling sad, disappointed, and rejected. This was an event in my middle school years that would forever follow me. Mama, do you have a similar memory of being bullied? One that you wish could be erased entirely from your memory bank? I can still remember it clear as day, and if asked, I am sure my classmates would recall it as well. "Remember the time..."

My life had its fair share of hard knocks; however, I can say now with absolute confidence that I am thankful for those who persecuted me because it has made me the fierce, motivated, fearless woman I am today. The tough times in my life only made me stronger. Overcoming the fear of what others thought of me allowed me to learn who I truly am outside of the viewpoints of this world. I don't strive to fit in as an adult because God says I am set apart, chosen, loved, and accepted.

Though I didn't see it at that moment, I now realize the behavior of the girls who made fun of me was driven by their own internal pain. Hurting people hurt other people. They project their own feelings of insecurity and brokenness onto others. They find easy targets—girls who won't fight back—and release their anger onto innocent victims. Hurting others makes them feel good and redirects their pain away from themselves. That doesn't make it right, and we don't have to carry the weight of their burdens. It just helps us to understand the person and their motives.

Unfortunately, there will be times when our daughters deal with mean girls. The more we talk with them about the heart of a mean girl, the better we can help them understand the hurt thrown at them. We can teach our daughters that the way people treat them or what they say about them has nothing to do with who they are. In fact, it says more about the person trying to cause the pain in the first place.

Instead of lashing out or turning inward, we can equip our girls to accept people for who they are—even when they treat them poorly. Forgive 7x70 (Matthew 18:21). Pray for them. If they are Jesus' followers, then our girls can find peace knowing that God is working in their hearts. Pray that God works in the spaces that are causing them to lash out and take their aggression out on our sweet daughters.

Consider it joy because these trials will shine a light on others who are hurting and allow us to love on them, even while they are attempting to hurt our girls. Bless, release, and give them to God. Walk away in confidence, knowing that this trial will only strengthen your daughter and allow her to develop into the beautiful God-girl He created.

GO DEEPER

Our Bible verse for today is easier said than done, right? Love your enemy. But what if they have a laundry list of pain they have caused? How could you possibly love them? The Passion Translation states, "Bless the one who curses you, do something wonderful for the one who hates you, and respond to the very ones who persecute you by praying for them. For that will reveal your identity as children of your heavenly Father. What reward do you deserve if you only love the loveable? Don't even the tax collectors do that? How are you any different from others if you limit your kindness only to your friends? Don't even the ungodly do that? Since you are children of the perfect Father in heaven, become perfect like Him." Matthew 6:44-48

Each day we should strive to be more like Jesus. Will we become perfect? Will we always get it right? Probably not, but we can do our best to lay down the bitterness and resentment and try.

Let's love our persecutors like the creation God made them be. That's tough and not an easy call to action. However, it will feel good in our souls when we get this right. The hurt that was caused suddenly goes away when we give it to God and love them where they are in their own pain.

Some people may contribute to our daughters' brokenness, highlighting insecurities they already feel about themselves. Give it all to God, love. He will meet you both in that brokenness and renew her identity in Him. James 1:3 says that "the testing of your faith (and girl, this is definitely a test) will produce perseverance." The suffering and pain that others cause will grow your faith in God. It's in those moments that we have an invitation to rebuke any lies that the enemy might feed us and allow God to reveal His truth in our hearts.

Reflect

*W*ere you ever bullied growing up? If so, what was that like? Have you ever considered what might have been going on in your persecutor's life? Write out a prayer of forgiveness.

If your daughter has been mistreated, write out a prayer for her persecutor as well. Give it to God and forgive. Don't forget to share that prayer with her.

♥ *Conversation Starters* ♥

Together, create a prayer list for those who persecute your girl. I know this is not easy, mama. But this is a tremendous opportunity for you and your girl to comb through past hurts and perhaps help her better understand the root cause of why someone is mistreating her. God can turn this to good when we allow Him to work in her pain and suffering.

Next, take a few moments to pray over the girls (perhaps even boys) she has listed.

Pray

Father God, thank You for reminding me that the suffering and pain others have caused my daughter and me isn't our burden to carry. Help me to love our enemies despite the hurt they have inflicted. Lord, I pray for them, their hearts, and whatever it might be that makes them feel the need to contribute to the brokenness of others. Renew my spirit, Lord. Create a spirit of forgiveness in me.
In Jesus' name, I pray. Amen.

Day 19

Steadfast: Denying the Invitation to be the Mean Girl

Therefore, my beloved brothers, be steadfast, immovable, always abounding in the work of the Lord, knowing that in the Lord your labor is not in vain.

1 Corinthians 15:58 NIV

As a quiet observer, I saw the dynamics of my school. There were the popular kids, the nerds, the alternative kids, and the in-betweeners. That last category was the one I fit into most—the in-betweener. I wasn't popular, I wasn't nerdy, I was just well...in-between. I flew under the radar, unnoticed most of the time. However, deep down inside, there was a growing awareness of what it meant to be popular. It meant I needed to dress in the best clothes, be exclusive in my friendships, and radiate a vibe that didn't sit well in my heart. A vibe that said, "I am better than you, prettier than you, skinnier than you, richer than you, and more athletic than you." Despite my desire to fit in with the popular crowd, I realized that it came with a cost: It often meant being a mean girl.

Chances are, at some point, our girls will have an opportunity to be the mean girl. Their need to feel loved and accepted may tempt them to cross from kind to cruel. Moments will present themselves when they have a split decision to make. Will they give in to pressure from the popular kids to purposefully leave out someone considered not cool? When they are around certain people, will they choose to carry a persona that isn't really who they are? An aura that says, "I am better than you, and I will protect that heart posture at all costs"?

Friend, because they have Jesus in their heart, a choice to be mean won't feel right. When they feel that sense of wrong within their heart, teach them to trust that the Holy Spirit is speaking and encourage them to follow His guidance.

No matter what pressures they face, God will give them the strength to resist temptation.

When our sweet girls place their trust in Him in all areas of their life, they will have peace. A peace that will outweigh any desire to fit in.

GO DEEPER

The Merriam-Webster dictionary says that steadfast means: "1: firmly fixed in place: immovable 2: not subject to change." The Passion Translation states, "Live your lives with an **unshakeable** confidence" 1 Corinthians 15:58. Where should that confidence come from... God, of course. When our daughter's faith is so deeply rooted in confidence in who she is in Christ, she won't need to take any other action to secure that confidence. It's already hers.

As Jesus followers, we can show our gratitude to our Father by standing firm in our faith and living in likeness to Him. Hebrews 12:28 TPT, "Since we are receiving our rights to an unshakeable kingdom, we should be extremely thankful and offer God the purest of worship that delights His heart as we lay down our lives in absolute surrender, filled with awe." Whatever we do in word or deed (Colossians 3:17) should be Holy and pleasing to God. When we remain unshakeable and downright immovable in our faith, when we refuse to fall prey to Satan's schemes, we are glorifying our Heavenly Father.

Let's allow God to direct our steps and give our hearts and choices to Him. He will provide us with the strength to be unmovable. When our girls are tempted to be the mean girl, it won't sit right in their hearts. When it doesn't feel right, they will refuse to act on that temptation and allow the enemy to use them to hurt others.

Reflect

How did you overcome the pressure to be the mean girl growing up? Did you ever feel the Holy Spirit guiding you regarding staying true to who you were? How can you encourage your girl to do the same?

♥ Conversation Starters ♥

Have you ever been given an invitation to be the mean girl? What did that feel like? Did you feel a heart pull one way or another? Have you acted on that decision before? Do you feel guilty about hurting someone? Pray together. Ask for God's forgiveness and invite Him to help mend that relationship. Encourage your daughter to consider approaching the girl and asking her for forgiveness.

Pray

Father God, give my daughter the courage to remain steadfast and true to her character despite the temptation to be mean to fit in. Help her to stand confident in who she is so that she chooses to be immovable when the opportunity presents itself to be anyone else. Lord, give her a spirit of love. Help her choose love over hatred. Give her the courage to find opportunities to be a light in a hurting world. When she witnesses others being hateful, lead, guide, and direct her to take a stand. In Jesus' name, I pray. Amen.

Day 20

Servant Heart: Loving Others from a Place of Love

For I am convinced that neither death nor life, neither angels nor demons, neither the present nor the future, nor any powers, neither height nor depth, nor anything else in all creation, will be able to separate us from the love of God that is in Christ Jesus our Lord.

Romans 8:38-39 NIV

I've always been a girl who feels big. When others hurt, I physically hurt too. My heart aches. Empathy is something I feel deep within my soul and always have. That song, "Break my heart for what breaks Yours," by Matthew West is a perfect description of my heart posture. Carrying the heart of Jesus. It makes perfect sense now that I think of it. God lives within me; the Holy Spirit leads me through this life. The heartbreak I feel for others is purposefully planted by God Himself.

However, I felt unworthy for most of my tween/teen years. Those feelings of worthlessness made it seem like I was unlovable and like I had nothing to offer to anyone else. That was a lie straight from the enemy himself. He wanted nothing more than to squash the love I had to give. In those younger years, I can remember time and time again that God had placed a sense of empathy within my heart and a call to act, but I didn't have the courage to follow through. Who was I? No one cares about me or what I have to say. The enemy kept me silent. He didn't want me to share God's light, so his lies spewed all over me, keeping me from acting on God's behalf.

Your daughter has love to give too, but, just as he did to me, Satan is doing his best to convince her that she isn't loved and that she has nothing to offer. Mama, you know this isn't true. You know she is loved because you love her with all your heart. With adoring eyes, you see her beauty and her potential, and you gleam with pride over who God made her to be. We have studied God's unfailing love over the past 20 days. We know that His love is steadfast and endures forever. His love for your daughter began the moment He created her in your womb. There's nothing she can do to make God love her more, and there's nothing she can do to make Him love her less.

So how can you prevent Satan's lies from penetrating her sweet soul? One of the biggest things you can do is teach her to take captive every thought that doesn't align with the love God promises.

Keep in mind that if she's lived for quite some time believing that she isn't worthy of being loved, it may take a while for her to feel she is. Give it time, and trust that as she realigns her thoughts and feelings about love, her experience will gradually change, and she will become free to give love. How will she know whom and how to love? The Holy Spirit lives in her, and because He does, He will show her the love needs of others. As a bonus, somehow, she will find that when she takes the pressure off herself to gain love and chooses instead to extend love, she is the one who will receive some of the biggest blessings.

I hope that by the time you are finished with this study, your daughter will live in absolute assurance that God loves her more than she could ever imagine. More than anyone on this planet could love her. She is the daughter of the King, and she is destined for absolute greatness. God loves her so much that He sent His Son to die for her, and I hope that knowing this encourages and empowers her to share in that glorious love.

GO DEEPER

"Our love for others is our grateful response to the love God first demonstrated to us"

1 John 4:19 TPT.

Have you ever encountered the love of Jesus? Maybe it was a promise fulfilled or a dream that one day He would restore your broken heart. Or He sent a friend to share a word of encouragement with you. Perhaps a prodigal walked away, but they returned fully restored and whole again. The love of Jesus is hard to explain until you fully experience it for yourself. The awestruck wonder and total humility of a love engulfs us like none other.

If you've experienced that for yourself, don't you want others to have the same type of divine appointment? You matter, your words matter; if God put a call to action on your heart to love someone, it's for a reason. Have the courage to act on His behalf. You might be surprised by the response you get. 1 John 4:11 TPT, "If He loved us with such tremendous love, then 'loving one another should be our way of life!'"

There is nothing, no nothing, that can separate us from God's love. As Romans 8:38-39 says, life will throw us our fair share of hard knocks, but we do not have to be victims of our circumstances. When we stand confident in God's love regardless of what comes our way, loving others becomes effortless.

Reflect

Do you and your daughter know your daughter's love language? If not, she can take a quick quiz online at https://www.5lovelanguages.com/quizzes/teen-quiz/ to discover how she best receives love (such as through quality time, physical affection, acts of service, etc.). This information can better equip you to love her the way she needs most.

Write out some ways to show her love based on the findings of the love language quiz.

♥ Conversation Starters ♥

When do you feel loved? Have you ever experienced the love of Jesus? If so, how did that feel? How could you extend that same love to someone else? Is there anyone in your life who could benefit from hearing about how much Jesus loves them? If so, who are they? What could you do to help them feel loved this week?

Pray

Father God, thank You for the reminder that my daughter doesn't have to believe the lies that tell her she is unlovable. When she feels unloved, remind her who she is: a daughter bought and paid for with a price and loved so much that You willingly died on the cross for her. Help her stand confident in that love so that she can serve and love others as You have loved her. Give me the eyes to see her need to feel loved and accepted. Give me the words to speak life and truth into her soul. In Jesus' name, I pray. Amen.

Day 21

Have Courage: Standing Up for What is Right

He has shown you, O mortal, what is good.
And what does the Lord require of you?
To act justly and to love mercy
and to walk humbly with your God.

Micah 6:8 NIV

I'll never forget a particular classmate who was bullied for much of her school-age years. Over and over, I witnessed other students teasing and taunting her. Each offense against this girl chipped away at my heart, but I didn't dare to stand up for her. What would happen if I said something? Would the mean girls retaliate against me? I hurt for her and couldn't imagine what she must be feeling. One day in gym class during my senior year of high school, I had finally seen enough. One last dig made me fuming mad. As I stood in the middle of the forming crowd, I told the bullies to pick on someone their own size. What I thought might happen did, but suddenly it didn't matter. They turned their aggression on me and questioned who I thought I was. I can remember the words to this day: "Who do you think you are, Miss Thang?" Somehow, their comeback didn't matter because I felt victory. For a split second, their attention wasn't on the girl they had targeted for years but, instead, was on me—and to my surprise, I was okay with it. The offenders might think twice before they went after her again.

Your daughter might witness things that don't sit well with her. When others mistreat someone, she might feel a heart tug like the one I felt for my classmate—the kind of heart tug we've talked about in previous days. When she feels that Holy Spirit whisper, God is telling her to move on the victim's behalf. It may not be easy. She may feel intimidated, but when she acts in obedience on someone's behalf, God will be right there with her, giving her the courage to stand up for what is right.

No one deserves to be treated poorly. When we find strength in our conviction to act according to God's will, we become the change in someone's circumstances. When we call out what is wrong, we invite the bullies to reconsider their attacks in the future. Let's encourage our girls to be strong and courageous, sis. They can do hard things and be someone's hero today. What a beautiful sight that will be.

GO DEEPER

"Speak up for those who cannot speak for themselves, for the rights of all who are destitute. Speak up and judge fairly; defend the rights of the poor"

Proverbs 31:8-9 NIV.

God calls us to intercede when we witness injustice. It's our duty as Jesus followers to ensure that people are treated fairly, lovingly, with grace and mercy. When others don't have the strength or courage to stand up for themselves, we can be their voice, ensuring that justice is won on their behalf.

Perhaps one of the best ways Jesus stood up for someone in the New Testament was when the Pharisees brought in a woman caught in adultery (John 8:3). The Pharisees questioned Jesus in hopes of trapping Him, 'Teacher, this woman was caught in the act of adultery. The Law of Moses commanded us to stone such women. Now, what do you say?' John 8:4 Jesus's response, 'Let any one of you who is without sin be the first to throw a stone at her.' She was speechless, unable to defend herself. By Jewish law, she had the right to be stoned, but Jesus entered, and everything changed. The Pharisees suddenly had no supporting arguments. They were all sinners themselves.

In Micah 6:8, God reveals that His requirements of us are to do what is right in His eyes, to be merciful toward others, and to be humble, submitting to Him and His plans. We get to be God's vessel for change when we walk in obedience in these areas. Just think what it might be like for your girl to intercede for someone who is hurting. She could be God's rescue plan for their life. Let's inspire her to stand in that confidence today.

Reflect

*I*s there someone in your daughter's life who could use a hero? If so, who is it?

Could you help spur your daughter on in being the voice and rescue plan for this person?

♥ Conversation Starters ♥

Ask that God guide you in standing up for anyone who might be mistreated this week. What will give you the courage to follow through and take this step? After talking, pray with your girl that she might have eyes to see the needs of others this week.

_____

_____

_____

_____

_____

_____

_____

_____

_____

_____

_____

_____

_____

_____

_____

_____

_____

_____

_____

_____

_____

_____

_____

_____

TRUDY LONESKY

Pray

Dear Heavenly Father, give my girl the eyes to see and the courage to act when she witnesses injustice. God, convict her heart and encourage her to be someone's hero today. What a privilege it is to be Your disciple. We get to be Your hands and feet. Help her be obedient to all the ways you call her to express justice, mercy, and humility. I know you've commanded these things, and I want nothing more than for her to be obedient in that call. In Jesus' name, I pray. Amen.

Day 22

Where are These Feelings Coming From? : Equipping Her to Honor Her Feelings

Trust in the LORD with all your heart and lean not on your own understanding; in all your ways submit to him, and he will make your paths straight.

Proverbs 3:5-6 NIV

Our girls are developing and growing into the beautiful beings God has created. There will be emotions and feelings they may find difficult to explain in all that growth and sometimes awkwardness. They could go about their day feeling happy and content when a wave of emotion suddenly hits them and sends them into an emotional tailspin.

This is oh-so-very normal and will carry on well into adulthood. You can help your girl recognize her feelings. Encourage her to take a moment to realize they are there and that they are valid. Help her learn to process them by asking herself questions: Are these feelings true, noble, kind? What zapped my joy? Did someone look at me a certain way? Was I scrolling through social media and suddenly felt as if I was left out, uninvited? Did someone's filtered version of perfection leave me feeling unworthy or not enough? Did I see another girl and compare myself with her?

Here are some words that may help your daughter describe what she is feeling:

- Happy
- Sad

- Angry
- Afraid
- Lonely
- Jealous
- Disgusted
- Surprised
- Anxious
- Unworthy

We can show our daughters how to honor their feelings by the way we honor ours. As mamas, we can do this by verbally processing our feelings aloud for our girls to hear. If, as we process, we realize that our emotions are happening because we are comparing ourselves to others or criticizing ourselves, we can adjust what we are focusing on to shift our feelings. As author Tony Robbins says, "Where focus goes, energy flows." As we process and refocus, our daughters might be better able to do the same.

Encourage your daughter to take her feelings to God. Instead of allowing the enemy to have his way in her emotional life, what if she asks God about her feelings? For example, she could pray, "Lord, I feel like I just don't belong. I saw that my friends had a party, and I wasn't invited. Will I ever fit in?" She can trust that God will deliver an answer. God is a God of provision, and that means He will always provide her every need. If she needs help processing her feelings, she can allow God to help her see where those feelings are coming from and how to deal with them appropriately.

GO DEEPER

In Jeremiah 17:9 NIV, it states, "The heart is deceitful above all things and beyond cure. Who can understand it?" If left to their own devices, our hearts can and will deceive us. Especially if we are coming from a place of irrational thought. Sometimes our thoughts and emotions can be so strong that we don't even understand where the feelings are coming from.

Verse 10 continues with, "I the Lord search the heart and examine the mind, to reward each person according to their conduct, according to what their deeds deserve." God knows our hearts, and He calls us to lay down the knee-jerk reactions, thoughts, and emotions and process our feelings through His biblical perspectives and truths.

"Trust in the LORD with all your heart and lean not on your own understanding; in all your ways submit to him, and he will make your paths straight"

Proverbs 3:5-6 NIV.

This is one of my very favorite verses in the Bible. When we are fully and completely, with all our heart, trusting in God and His will, we take the pressure off ourselves and others. When we take away the weight of understanding the world through our own deceptive eyes and instead "lean" on God (that means to put all our weight, both physically and emotionally, on Him), we give Him permission to help us process, honor, and then move to a godly understanding of our emotions.

Our girls don't have to remain bound by their feelings of anger, sadness, loneliness, not enough, worthlesness, unloved, or uninvited because God hasn't given her a spirit of fear or condemnation. These burdens aren't meant for her to carry.

Reflect

*A*re there times when your daughter seems hot-tempered? Sometimes our daughters take things out on us because we are a safe space. Honor that space. In the space below, jot down some ideas about how you can help your daughter process the next meltdown.

♥ *Conversation Starters* ♥

What strategy can you put in place with your girl to help her process her feelings? Is it taking a deep breath? Is it going to be a quiet place? Is it praying? Is it providing her with a safe space to vent all her frustrations? Is it playing praise and worship music really loud? Take some time to encourage her to process her thoughts and feelings and give her a space to do so whenever she needs.

_____

_____

_____

_____

_____

_____

_____

_____

_____

_____

_____

_____

_____

_____

_____

_____

_____

_____

_____

_____

_____

_____

_____

_____

Pray

Father God, give me the patience and courage to allow my girl to process her feelings when they are all-consuming. Give me the eyes to see the buildup of emotions before they explode, Lord. When I see she is overwhelmed, prompt me to be a safe place for her to process. Give me a gentle spirit and help me be a calming presence when she needs it most.
In Jesus' name, I pray. Amen.

Day 23

Bad Days: How She Can Honor Them

Because of the Lord's great love we are not consumed,
for his compassions never fail.
They are new every morning;
great is your faithfulness.

Lamentations 3:22-23 NIV

Your daughter will have good days, but she will also have bad days—terrible, awful, I-cannot-face-the-world days. There will be times when she arrives at school with a big stain on her shirt, or she will forget her science project or her soccer cleats. She will have bad hair days (for the 1980s era me, a bad hair day meant the poof wasn't high enough or the Aqua Net wasn't doing its thing.... Yes, I was that girl), tired days, and she-just-can't-even days. Days when her boyfriend breaks up with her and her eyes are so swollen from the ugly cry that she can't bear the thought of going out in public. There will be days when she doesn't even want to get out of bed.

You can inspire her to face her difficulties and do it anyway. There's something powerful about laughing in the face of those horrific days, calling them for what they are, picking yourself up, and dusting yourself off. Bad days only persist if we allow them to. Teach her to honor the bad and accept it for what it is, and get out of the head funk and reposition her mindset.

What's something she can do to change her focus among utter disappointment? What brings her joy? Could she paint her nails, draw, read, bake, go outside for a walk, listen to music, or sing ridiculously loudly and pretend she has just been "found?" Could you invite her BFF over for ice cream and allow her to vent?

Don't allow her to stay stuck. There's no fun in wallowing in sadness. Empower her to get out of her own head and focus on the blessings in her life. There are far too many to count. She can do hard things, and she can do far more with a rockstar mama like you. Tomorrow is a whole new day.

GO DEEPER

James 1:2 NIV, "Consider it *pure* joy, my brothers and sisters, whenever we face trials of many kinds." Hold up. Joy is not something we would use to describe a difficult day. How could we possibly process all the yuckiness by being joyful? Here's how. "Because you know that the testing of your faith produces perseverance" James 1:3. We can see the terrible, awful as a testing of our faith, realign our thought process, and ask God how He sees the situation.

Let's keep going; this is getting good. Verse 4 says, "Let perseverance finish its work so that you may be mature and complete, not lacking *anything.*" So, we can use the bad and turn it to good just like God promises (Romans 8:28)? Yes, yes, we can. When we persevere, we grow mature in our faith. This is where we experience the faithfulness of our Lord and Savior.

Wait, there's more. Verse 5, "If any of you lacks wisdom, you should ask God, who gives generously to *all* without finding fault, and it will be given to you." How many times do our bad days have us wondering why? Girl, what if we ask God why? Shew! It's there that He promises to give us that wisdom we so longingly desire to have.

In Lamentations 3:22-23, Jeremiah reminds us that our hope lies in the Lord and His promises. Each day brings new mercies, healing, and redemption. Our daughters don't have to stay in the circumstances they have been given because we have a good, good Father Who promises to make her new in Him. She can rest in faith that the bad days won't last. She doesn't have to be consumed with her disappointments because each new day brings mercy, grace, peace, and joy. Encourage her to fix her eyes on Him, sweet sister. He is where our hope is found.

Reflect

hat strategies can you come up with in advance to handle the bad days your girl will be given? Is it a girls' day out? A spa day? A manicure and pedicure? A hike? A dance party in your kitchen? What brings her joy and will help her get out of the messy headspace?

♥ *Conversation Starters* ♥

What things bring you pure joy? What are some things we can do together as mother and daughter to help you through a difficult day?

TRUDY LONESKY

Pray

Father God, I thank You for Your promises. I thank You that Your mercies are made new every single morning. When my girl's weary heart keeps her in cycles of destructive thought patterns, Lord, remind her that she has a choice to stay there or stay grounded in Your truth. Thank You for loving her where she is. Thank You for the many blessings You have given us. Thank You for this awakening and realignment. In Jesus' name, I pray. Amen.

Day 24

Style and Grace-Finding Beauty in Modesty

Instead, it should be that of your inner self, the unfading beauty of a gentle and quiet spirit, which is of great worth in God's sight.

1 Peter 3:4 NIV

"She was beautiful, but not like those girls in the magazines. She was beautiful, for the way she thought. She was beautiful for the sparkle in her eyes when she talked about something she loved. She was beautiful for her ability to make people smile, even if she was sad. No, she wasn't beautiful for something as temporary as her looks. She was beautiful, deep down to her soul." F Scott Fitzgerald

Thumbing through the pages of **Teen Magazine**, I daydreamed of being able to pull off the skimpy crop tops, bikinis, and short shorts celebrities wore. As a teenager, I spent so much energy wishing I looked good in these kinds of clothing. *If I looked this good, then maybe, just maybe, I would fit in,* I reasoned. Somehow, my mom's handmade clothes just didn't quite compare to the designer labels. Perhaps I could slip her a new sewing pattern with a little less fabric?

As a teenager, I didn't understand what modesty was or why it mattered. But I now know that modesty means honoring our bodies by covering them properly. It means choosing clothing that covers areas we wish to remain unseen. Modesty matters because being modest honors God shows respect for ourselves and makes it more likely that others will respect us. Let's help our daughters understand the value of modesty. Let's help them understand that being beautiful is not about wearing revealing clothing. As mothers, the way we dress will set a standard for our daughters. When we choose clothing that honors God, our bodies, and those around us, our daughters get to witness that small act of obedience.

We can encourage our girls to shine bright and beautiful no matter their clothing choices because the light they shine is not a light of the world but a light that only Jesus can give—a radiance that glistens from the inside out. In fact, as Jesus followers, we have a great responsibility to walk in a way that looks different from the way others walk. Our body is a temple. God's temple. The moment we ask Jesus into our hearts, the Holy Spirit enters our bodies and lives in us. That makes us holy and should convict us to live accordingly.

Have you ever seen a beautiful person who radiates and shines? One who could wear an oversized sweatshirt, baggy sweatpants, zero make up and be absolutely stunning? I have! And I know that radiant beauty comes from something that money can't buy. It comes from quiet, humble confidence in who you are. It comes from forgetting who the world says you are and ignoring the status quo in your clothing choices. It comes from having complete faith and reliance on God's unfailing love and acceptance.

Our daughters can dress classy and still be radiant. In fact, it's that class and "Godfidence" that makes her shine above all else. Let's empower her to embrace that kind of confidence. We see it in her. Now it's time for her to see it too.

GO DEEPER

Our bodies are temples, God living within us. It's our call as Jesus' girls to honor and glorify Him by the way we carry ourselves. Not falling into the patterns of this world and the way it dresses but submitting our clothing choices to Him. 1 Corinthians 6:19-20 NIV says, "Or do you not know that your body is a temple of the Holy Spirit within you, whom you have from God? You are not your own, for you were bought with a price. So, glorify God in your body." Our bodies were bought with an expensive price, Jesus dying on the cross for us. That's weighty and heavy. It's in that reverence and respect for His ultimate sacrifice that we should find it necessary to honor Him. Laying down the need to show extra skin or dress in a way that isn't pleasing to God.

In 1 Peter 3:3, "Your beauty should not come from outward adornment." Here's our call to lay down the desire to glorify ourselves by the way we dress. Instead, Peter instructs us to be focused on inner beauty rather than outward appearance. Inner beauty comes from a place of love. Loving yourself as the creation God has made and loving others. When we nurture a relationship with Jesus and spend time with Him, inner beauty will shine. We will radiate love, peace, joy, mercy, and grace in their highest forms when we allow God to transform our hearts from the inside out. True beauty is found within the heart.

Reflect

*H*ow can you encourage your girl to dress modestly? Are there stores that provide good clothing choices? Are there some that you need to encourage her to stay away from?

♥ Conversation Starters ♥

If you were to meet Jesus at a local bakery for a cupcake or coffee, what would you wear? Are there some items in your closet you wouldn't feel comfortable wearing in front of Him? Take some time to go through your closet and purge or donate items that do not glorify God.

Pray

Father God, I pray over my girl. Please give her the courage to love herself regardless of the clothing she wears. May she radiate confidence and that she no longer feels the need to wear clothing that reveals too much of her body. Lord, convict her when she is tempted to overstep. Fill her from the inside out. In that fullness, she will lay down any need to find identity or worth in her clothing choices.
In Jesus' name, I pray. Amen.

Day 25

Emboldened: Your Daughter's Voice Matters

Don't let anyone look down on you because you are young, but set an example for the believers in speech, in conduct, in love, in faith and in purity.

1 Timothy 4:12 NIV

When I was a student, popcorn reading—an exercise in which teachers would make each student take turns reading assigned paragraphs out loud—was my nemesis. Do you remember doing that in school? Whenever my class had to do it, I would skip ahead and count how many paragraphs until it was my turn. I skimmed the section assigned to me, hoping there weren't any words I couldn't pronounce. One day in fifth-grade social studies, what I always feared happened. I was assigned a paragraph and mispronounced the word "determined." I said, "deter-mined." Immediately, a boy in my class called me out. He laughed at my mistake, inviting the rest of the class to snicker with him. It stung. At that moment, I wished I could crawl under my desk and hide there for eternity.

Events like this made me believe I was stupid and made me think that no one would ever care about what I had to say. How could I influence anyone, especially those who seemed to have it all together? Satan is sneaky, seeking to steal, kill, and destroy. He filled me with lies, but God eventually revealed the truth: There were lots of people who cared about what I had to say. There were people who valued who I was as a person. I'm so glad God helped me see this because, if He hadn't, I would have missed out on so much, including writing this book!

In 1 Timothy 4:12, Paul says, "Don't let anyone look down on you because you are young."

When people act rudely and look down on our girls, they might think they have nothing to offer. But the truth is, they have influence. Regardless of their age, abilities, or personality, what they have to say matters. We shouldn't allow our girls to look down on themselves or let the opinion of others hold them back. They will do immeasurable things because God lives in them. It's time for our daughters to embrace all that God has put before them.

For instance, God might call them to be leaders, even when they don't feel equipped. That might include being a captain on a sports team or leading a devotion at youth group. Our girls can trust that God sees their potential, that God has placed opportunities in front of them for a reason, and that He will provide everything they need to succeed in those leadership roles.

Your daughter has influence, mama because Christ lives in her. She has a calling to shine the light that He radiates in and through her. Empower your sweet girl to be bold enough to live out that confidence so others can't help but want the joy, peace, and love she so confidently shares.

GO DEEPER

David, a hero of his time, was what people would consider young when he heard God's call to deliver the Israelites from the Philistine giant, Goliath. Experts say he was around 13-15 years of age.

1 Samuel 17:33 NIV, "Saul replied, 'You are not able to out against this Philistine (Goliath) and fight him; you are only a young man, and he has been a warrior from his youth.'" While the rest of the army stood around and froze in fear, David felt God's call to action on his heart. It was his faith that caused David to take action, "The Lord who rescued me from the paw of the lion and the paw of the bear (while tending sheep) will rescue me from the hand of this Philistine," 1 Samuel 17:37 NIV. Talk about bold faith and the strength to stand. While Goliath mocked and taunted David, David replied, "You come against me with sword and spear and javelin, but I come against you in the name of the Lord Almighty," 1 Samuel 17:45 NIV.

"As the Philistine moved closer to attack him, David ran quickly toward the battle line to meet him," 1 Samuel 17:48 NIV. David wasn't afraid of Goliath. He was fearless because God gave him courage and tenacity. David struck the giant down with one stone and a slingshot. The odds were against David, but one thing made him mightier than a giant ever could be, and that was the God who lived within him. David is called "a man after God's own heart." David gave all fear to God. He surrendered his whole heart to Him.

God can use our girls in the same way He used David. We don't have to put limitations on them because they are young. If God has placed a call on their lives, it's for His good and perfect plan.

In 1 Timothy 4:12, Paul encourages us to remember that just because we are young doesn't mean we can't be the change we want to see in this world. Your girl can have an impact just by living differently than others—by not allowing her circumstances to hold her back, by choosing joy in the face of adversity. No matter her age, she has a calling on her life as a Jesus girl. That calling is to live so confidently in who she is that it inspires others to walk in faith alongside her.

Reflect

*W*hat leadership qualities do you see in your daughter? Where has God called her to be a leader in school and in your community? How do you see God using her in the future to influence those around her?

♥ Conversation Starters ♥

Share the answers that you wrote in the journal portion above with your daughter. Tell her how you see God's leadership qualities in her. Together, brainstorm a way for her to be a godly influence on those around her. Some ideas might include initiating a prayer group or Bible study before school, leaving post-it notes on lockers with words of encouragement, or making friendship bracelets and sharing them with classmates.

Pray

Father God, thank You for the calling and purpose You have placed over my daughter's life. When she feels ill-equipped, remind her that she has influence because You have given her favor. Help her walk confidently in faith, live out her purpose, and be the change we all want to see in this world. Lord, open her eyes to see the needs of others and encourage her to act in faith to meet those needs. In Jesus' name, I pray. Amen.

Day 26

Today is a Gift: Time Management

So, teach us to number our days that we may get a heart of wisdom.

Psalm 90:12 NIV

For most of my life, time management has been a struggle. Enneagram 7 here. I want to do all the things. I have lofty ideas and want to do it all. Focus is hard for me. More often than I'd like to admit, I get distracted and end up waiting until the last minute to finish an assignment or a project, sweating and squirming to crunch the time I have left. Sometimes, I'm not able to create my best work because I don't allow myself enough time to do so. Leaving myself feeling like I should have used my time more effectively.

As hard as it can be, I know that managing our time matters because God says our days here on earth are numbered. We can honor God by how we spend our time, and a great place to start doing so is by asking ourselves these questions: Are we productive in our daily lives? Do we let distractions (what I like to call "squirrels"—picture Doug in the movie *Up*) derail us? Do we spend time and attention on what matters most? What should matter most, anyway? God, of course. He should be front and center in our lives. I've found that once He is my priority, all other areas in my life fall into place.

Just as we do, our children live in a world competing for their attention. If we don't teach them to guard their time and focus, it will get away from them, and they will fail to focus on what matters most. One day, your daughter will have a job. By learning to manage her time wisely now, she will set herself up for success in the workplace. God will work in and through her life, blessing her for her obedience when she takes pride in her work to glorify Him. Encourage your daughter to honor God and His plans in her life by doing the very best she can. We are a reflection of Him wherever we go.

GO DEEPER

1 Peter 4:2-3 TPT, "²So live the rest of your earthly life no longer concerned with human desires but consumed with what brings pleasure to God." We get to honor God with our time by using the talents and gifts He has given us for effective use. If we procrastinate on a big assignment or run late for work, we aren't honoring God. We can model what a good steward of our time being looks like for our girls. Strategically helping them plan out their week, their assignments, how to manage schoolwork and sports, and a job.

Peter goes on to say in verse 3, "³For you have already spent enough time doing what unbelievers do." Getting caught up by distractions of this world like scrolling social media or binge-watching Netflix, or even playing video games steals our time and attention away from what matters most to God. Which is using what He's given us, taking our work seriously, spending time with Him in His word, studying the Bible, and intentionally learning and growing as Jesus followers.

Where we spend our time and energy matters. In Psalms 90:12, the Psalmist reminds us that God has numbered our days. He knows how we will spend those days. He's written our story already. He knows every minute detail. We can honor and show gratitude toward Him when we use our time to glorify Him and who He has created us to be.

Reflect

n what areas does your daughter need coaching in managing her time wisely? How can you help her organize her schoolwork, chores, and after-school activities?

♥ *Conversation Starters* ♥

How can I help you organize your time to use it better? In what areas of your life do you feel flustered because you lack the time necessary to finish a task well?

Pray

Father God, I know that You have numbered our days. Help me honor You by being intentional about how our family spends the hours in those days. Convict me when I spend my time in the wrong places and help me limit my distractions. In doing so, my daughter will see how to use her time effectively. Help my girl stay focused and determined to be the best version of herself by honoring the time You have given her. In Jesus' name, I pray. Amen.

Day 27

The Girl for the Job: Commitment and Follow Through

And whatever you do, whether in word or deed, do it all in the name of the Lord Jesus, giving thanks to God the Father through him.

Colossians 3:17 NIV

For years, I had to work for every little thing I had. But though those years were difficult, they built character and resilience within me. All those times my parents sent me off into the vegetable garden to pull weeds, or the times my dad asked me to help stack firewood only made me stronger, created a sense of pride and accomplishment, made me work harder, and developed discipline.

The late nights I spent scrubbing the oil fryers at the Abbot Town Line (our local ice cream shop), making sure everything was perfect and would pass my boss's white glove test, created work ethic, grit, and determination.

And the summers in college when I worked at the wool mill spinning wool into thread, dealing with malfunctioning machines, and feeling continually exhausted, helped me learn how to problem solve and keep calm while under pressure.

At times, working so hard seemed overwhelming, daunting, and unfair. Still, these experiences absolutely made me into the person I am in adulthood—a strong, empowered, motivated God girl who takes pride in completing the task at hand.

Mama, I am sure that as you look back on your life and the assignments you have been given, you can see how those tasks developed character and pride. Chances are, some of the most challenging jobs you had turned out to be the ones that taught you to persevere and overcome and showed you just how awesome you are.

When God calls your daughter to do a job, do a chore, volunteer, or even join a sports team, encourage her to take pride in what she's been asked to do. It doesn't matter how small the task at hand. God is sure to show up in a big way in whatever it is that He has called her to. Help her look for ways to flourish, grow, and learn through the opportunities she has been given.

GO DEEPER

Let's study the apostle Paul. A warrior for Christ. Unlikely to be called to disciple Jesus' people because he was the person who persecuted Christians. Saul (later renamed Paul by Jesus on the road to Damascus) was present during the stoning of Stephen. He would go on to persecute Christians for 3 years. Until his conversion, the moment he met Jesus on the Road to Damascus. Acts 9:3-4 NIV, "³As he neared Damascus on his journey, suddenly a light from heaven flashed around him. ⁴He fell to the ground and heard a voice say to him, 'Saul, Saul, why do you persecute me?'" It was there, a Jesus encounter that would forever change the trajectory of Saul's life. Transformed. Made new.

Paul, one of the biggest influences in founding the early church, was given an assignment by God himself. One that would forever change the landscape of Christianity. Spreading the gospel to the ends of the earth just like Jesus had commanded His disciples to do. The Great Commission. Instructions were given by Jesus to His disciples after His death and resurrection.

It wasn't a small task. His ministry lasted 35 years, beginning with his conversion in 33 AD. Expert biblical scholars agree that Paul traveled over 10,000 miles by foot. He was imprisoned 3 times for his tenacity in spreading the gospel and spent nearly five years in prison. Nevertheless, Paul was obedient and steadfast in God's call over his life. Paul was a mediator and advocate of Gentiles (that's you and me). He wrote 13 of the 27 books of the New Testament and was a martyr for the sake of the Gospel.

In the book of Colossians, Paul wrote to the church of Colossae while imprisoned in Rome. In Colossians 3:17, Paul encourages us to reflect on Christ in every detail of our daily lives. Shew! No pressure, right? This comes from a man who died as a martyr. One that professed his faith at all costs to his life. In all seriousness, though, if we too profess to be Christians, people watch how we live our lives. Do we carry our God-given assignments with obedience and faithfulness?

Reflect

*T*hink of opportunities you have had in the past. Were there God-given responsibilities that you weren't excited about tackling? How would that experience have been different if your heart had been in a place of honor and reverence for having an opportunity to be the hands and feet of Jesus? Does your girl have a sense of pride when it comes to the assignments God has given her? How might you be able to help her exhibit a sense of gratitude?

♥ Conversation Starters ♥

> What responsibilities are you grateful for? Are there some that you dread? How can we reposition our hearts to a posture of thankfulness to glorify God?

Pray

Father God, I thank You for the opportunities You have given my daughter to shine Your beautiful light. Thank You, Lord, for allowing us to be Your hands and feet all the days of our lives, in the big things and the little things. When opportunities present themselves to be Your servant, Lord, help us reposition our hearts to a heart of gratitude and praise. In Jesus' name, I pray. Amen.

Day 28

It's Okay to Say No: People Pleasing

For am I now seeking the approval of man or of God? Or am I trying to please man? If I were still trying to please man, I would not be a servant of Christ.

Galatians 1:10 NIV

For most of my life, I would go to any length for someone to like me, even if that meant crossing boundaries or exhausting myself. My answer to someone's request was almost always automatic: ***Yes! I'll do whatever I need to do for you to like me. I'm your girl.*** There was no pondering or thinking it over. No thinking about how that yes could affect me or someone else.

I learned later in life that when I say yes to something, 9 times out of 10, I am saying no to something else. In my adult life, my yes means that I am usually saying no to my family. When I agree to take on a responsibility that is beyond my capacity, I get stressed, short-circuited, and snippy. Leaving those closest to me the rest of me not the best of me. Eventually, I would learn that I would need to take time and consider the consequences of my yes. How would it affect my time, space, and energy? Would that take away from the things that already took precedence on my schedule? If I don't have the time in my schedule to commit to something with my whole heart, then the answer has to be no, and I had to learn it was okay.

Times may come when your daughter says yes without thinking. In her need to please people and find validation, she may be tempted to stray from that moral compass that God designed within her heart.

She might be asked to do things that don't fit within the boundaries God wants for her life. Maybe she will be asked to Juul, drink, or create an inappropriate TikTok. If it feels wrong, then it is wrong. No form of validation from making a poor decision will right the wrong. Remember how we talked about being steadfast and unwavering? Here's the chance for her to do that. Let's equip her with the courage to say no and politely walk away. The people who really love her and value her as a person will not require her to do anything that doesn't align with who she truly is or be anyone other than herself. They will love her for the beautiful person God created her to be.

There might also be times when the desire to please people will lead your daughter to participate in activities that aren't necessarily bad but may not be the best fit for her. She could be asked to join a club, play a sport, be on the student council, or take part in some other extracurricular activity that she doesn't really want to do. Yet, she might find it hard to say no because she feels obligated. She might feel afraid to let someone down if she says no. The next time she is asked to do something, invite her to rate that opportunity from one to five, with one being "I don't really want to do it" and five being "I can't wait to get started." If it's not a five, chances are she isn't meant to fill that role. Someone else will fill it, I promise.

I know it is tough to say no. Chances are, she is afraid that saying no will hurt someone's feelings. Let's encourage her to honor her God-given boundaries and her God-given time. Saying no can be freeing, giving her the space and time to spend on the things that she absolutely enjoys in life.

GO DEEPER

Proverbs 29:25 TPT, "Fear and intimidation is a trap that holds you back." The NLT translates this verse as, "Fearing people is a dangerous trap, but trusting the Lord means safety." Behind our need to say yes and please people is fear. Fear that if we say no to something, we will hurt feelings or someone will be upset with us. What if we give that fear to the Lord? There's a confidence in taking a moment to consider an ask, giving that to the Lord, and asking Him how He sees the opportunity fit in our lives. Fear is a liar and a trap, just as the verse states.

Are you seeking the approval of others or the approval of God? Sweet mama, there is peace in laying down the people-pleasing and resting in Him. It's not always easy to give that desire over to Him, but He will meet you where you are and fill that void with more love and adoration than you could ever imagine. When we lay down the desire to do it all and be everything we've been asked, we can better concentrate on God's highest in our lives. His priorities are at the top of that list. When we get this right, we can encourage our girls to do the same. Stand firm, friend; you can do hard things.

Reflect

*A*re you a people pleaser? Do you say yes to things that really aren't of interest to you? Pray about how you can politely decline an invitation to do something you don't really want to do. How can you encourage your girl to do the same?

♥ Conversation Starters ♥

> **What are some activities or obligations that, rather than filling you up, are making you feel drained? Can we consider letting those responsibilities go?**

_____

_____

_____

_____

_____

_____

_____

_____

_____

_____

_____

_____

_____

_____

_____

_____

_____

_____

_____

_____

_____

_____

_____

_____

_____

_____

Pray

Father God, help me lay down the need to please others. Lord, remind me it's okay to say no to honor You. My ultimate purpose in this life is to faithfully walk the path. You put before me. When I am asked to do something that doesn't align with Your purpose in my life, give me the courage to say no. Thank You for always being my guiding light. Please guide my girl in her decision making as well. When asked to do something, she has divine discernment in You. In Jesus' name, I pray. Amen.

Day 29

You Belong Here: Diversity

A new command I give you: Love one another. As I have loved you, so you must love one another. By this, everyone will know that you are my disciples if you love one another.

John 13:34-35 NIV

After graduating from college, I lived in the big city of Philadelphia and taught in what the locals call "Hell." As a small-town Maine girl, living in the city was a complete culture shock, but I loved my job as a teacher. I taught hundreds of students coming from rough areas. Many of the students never experienced a close relationship with a white person. This was my chance to love like Jesus. I was a safe space and a means of encouragement for my students.

Our girls will have opportunities to love people who don't look like them. I hope they are open to seeing those possibilities and dare to act on them, that they don't let differences in appearance or cultural background hold them back.

Jesus wasn't the blonde-haired, blue-eyed baby we sometimes see in paintings and pictures. His skin was olive, and He wore long hair and a beard. He looked different from what I do, and He might have looked different from you and your daughter do too. If Jesus were to go to school with your daughter, would she talk to Him if she didn't know He was Jesus? Would she invite Him to sit with her or have lunch with her? Would she help Him with His schoolwork?

God calls us to love others, period. He doesn't say to love those we choose to love. No, He challenges us to love everyone. In fact, when we open and invite someone in who doesn't necessarily look the way we do, we get to learn and grow through that process. Cultural differences don't mean we build walls. Cultural differences are an opportunity to build bridges and a chance to learn something new and beautiful.

Accepting others for who they are allows our daughters to go against the status quo. Their love is pure and kind. When they are a radiant light for all to see, not just the people they keep close to but everyone around them, they get to share God's love and do precisely what Jesus expects of them. When they act in love, they show others that they are Jesus' disciples, His hands, and feet.

Sweet mama, you won't find a person on this planet whom God doesn't love. He challenges us to do the same. Invite others in, lend a helping hand, and open the possibilities for new, life-giving friendships.

GO DEEPER

Acts 17:26 TPT, "From one man, Adam, he made every man and woman and every race of humanity, and he spread us over all the earth." When we see others as God's beautiful creation, it's easy to love them well. There's not a person on this planet that God didn't create and that He doesn't love. We can honor God and His creation by seeing them through the God who created them, perfectly in His image.

Galatians 3:28 TPT, "And we no longer see each other in our former state (enslaved or free)-Jew or non-Jew, rich or poor, male or female-because we're all one through our union with Jesus Christ." One big, happy family under the bloodline of Jesus. Doesn't that make you want to celebrate every human? This is a call to love our Jesus family well, no matter who they are or where they come from.

It's easy to love those who look and behave like us. It's challenging to step out of our comfort zone, be vulnerable, and love people who are different. But God made everyone beautifully unique. He loves every person, and He was purposeful when He created each one. We can show the love of Jesus when we set aside differences, break down barriers, and extend invitations. As a result, we will be known as Jesus' disciples. I can't think of a better label than that.

Reflect

What keeps you in your comfort zone? What barriers or walls have you built? What would it take for you to bring down those walls? How can you ask God to work in those spaces of vulnerability?

♥ Conversation Starters ♥

Is there a girl in your community whom you could extend love to? Someone who is easily overlooked and not invited? Could you invite her to the youth group? Or ask her to sit with you at lunch? Think of a way to extend love to her this week. It could be as simple as giving her a compliment.

Pray

Father God, I confess that it's easy to be comfortable in my circle of friends. Opening up to others who don't necessarily look like me is scary and uncomfortable. Challenge me to overcome those fears. Lord, open my eyes to see opportunities for me to be Your hands and feet. Show me where I need to extend love. Give me the courage to do so. Break my daughter's heart for those whom others have shut out. I pray she has the eyes and ears to see and hear ways that she can open up and extend love and invite others in. In Jesus' name, I pray. Amen.

Day 30

Social Media: A False Reality

The thief comes only to steal and kill and destroy. I came that they may have life and have it abundantly.

John 10:10 NIV

Social media—it's where everyone communicates and displays their best version of themselves. It's where we find out what people are doing, where they've been, and who they are hanging out with. The desire to be in the know has us grasping onto every form of social media out there—TikTok, Instagram, Snapchat, Facebook...

Social media is a huge part of our everyday lives. Because of it, your daughter can have a challenging time escaping bullying and other kinds of upsetting experiences. Not only is it harder to get away from mean kids, but social invites her to play the comparison game. Her feed is filled with highlight reels and pictures of filtered perfection. Rarely does she see real life. It's all a facade.

Social media also has a way of magnifying her feelings of being not enough, uninvited, and unseen. She could have her best day ever, but one quick peek at social, and her joy could be zapped in an instant. Maybe she sees a picture of her friends together at a sleepover that she wasn't invited to. Or she sees that a "friend" commented on her post and what they said was rude and distasteful. Even worse, she notices a "friend" deleted and blocked her.

Mama, let's not let our girls allow the effects of social media to determine their worth. Let's not let feelings of unworthiness and comparison penetrate her heart and her mind. They aren't meant to be there. The enemy wants her to feel less than and not enough. He seeks to steal, kill, and destroy, and social media is a perfect example of how the enemy uses people to destroy what God is creating within us. Jesus came so that we may have life, an abundant life filled with blessings and goodness.

Social is not and will never be real life. Social will never take the place of real, meaningful relationships and conversations. I hope your daughter has taken the time to find God girls to come alongside her and breathe life and truth into her sweet little being. Life-giving friendships that will help her see what's authentic and praiseworthy.

GO DEEPER

1 Timothy 6:6-7 TPT, "⁶We have a 'profit' that is greater than theirs-our holy awe of God! To have merely our necessities is to have enough. ⁷Isn't it true that our hands were empty when we came into the world and when we leave this world, our hands will be empty again?" Social might have us wishing we had more, were as beautiful, invited, enough. Rest on the fact that we have God in our lives, and He is enough. We can't take anything from this world. When we die, nothing but our souls will experience eternity.

Verse 9, "But those who crave the wealth of this world slip into spiritual snares. They become trapped by the troubles that come through their foolish and harmful desires, driven by greed and drowning in their own sinful pleasures. And they take others down with them into their corruption and eventual destruction." Social is a spiritual snare. It causes us to believe that we aren't enough. When we fall into comparison traps, we agree with the lies that Satan has spoken over us.

John 10:10 states that Jesus came to this earth to live an abundant life. Wikipedia says that "abundant life" means: "life in its abounding fullness of joy and strength for spirit, soul, and body. Abundant life signifies a contrast to feelings of lack, emptiness, and dissatisfaction, and such feelings may motivate a person to seek for the meaning of life and a change in their life." God came so that we could live life and live it to the full, not lacking anything. God needs to be our source of joy and peace. The enemy will do his best to distract our girls from these truths. Social can be Satan's ploy to destroy our confidence—but only if we allow it to be.

Reflect

Which social media outlet does your girl spend the most time on? Is it life-giving or life-taking? Have you observed her demeanor changing while using this app? Do you find that time slips away from her when she checks out and checks in to social media?

♥ Conversation Starters ♥

Do you compare yourself to others when you check in to social media? Do you find that time slips away when you check in? Do certain accounts steal your joy? Maybe it's time to unfollow accounts that do not fill you with joy and love.

Pray

Heavenly Father, open my eyes to see when my girl gets lost on social. When her weary heart compares herself to someone else's version of perfection, remind her that it's not real and that she doesn't need to feel less than. Lord, fill the need that drives her to seek approval from others on social. Remind her where she stands in Your eyes alone. Help her stand confident in Your truths and keep her from slipping into lies that she is not enough. When social takes time away from those, who matter most, convict her to lay it down at Your feet. In Jesus' name, I pray. Amen.

Conclusion

Beautiful friend,

I hope that this 30-day devotional was not only a journey of discovery for you as a mama but also as a woman of God. I hope you feel refreshed and have a renewed sense of peace and joy about God's plans for your life and for your family. Please promise me you won't stop here. Promise that you will continue to seek Him, dive deeper into the Bible, and find women to come alongside you to study His ways. It's my hope that you feel transformed and renewed in your relationship with your Heavenly Father and your baby girl. Might these last 30 days bring you newfound, godly confidence in parenting your sweet children. You can do hard things.

I love you, beautiful.
Reclaim your daughter of Zion. Fix her crown. You are the mom for the job.

Blessings,
Your sister in Christ

About the Author

Trudy is a mom of four, wife to Tim, and lover of Jesus. Born and raised in small-town Maine, now a resident of Kentucky. I am passionate about raising Jesus followers and cultivating authentic faith in the next generation. Author, podcaster, speaker, and mom to many. Living every day with Jesus, purpose, and spreading His love like confetti.